OKLAHOMA
CHEROKEE BASKETS

OKLAHOMA CHEROKEE BASKETS

KAREN COODY COOPER

THE History PRESS

Published by The History Press
Charleston, SC
www.historypress.net

Back cover: A toddler sits in a large Rachel Tanner buckbrush basket. *Carl Albert Center Congressional Archives, University of Oklahoma.*

First published 2016

Manufactured in the United States

ISBN 978.1.46711.982.5

Library of Congress Control Number: 2015960003

CONTENTS

ACKNOWLEDGEMENTS

This work is dedicated to Oklahoma Cherokee basket makers: past, present and future. Although American Indian basketry was generally women's craft in earlier times, this study also recognizes three men whose interest in American Indian basket history led me to write this book. I was working at the American Indian Archaeological Institute (now the Institute for American Indian Studies) in Washington, Connecticut, when I first met Claude Medford Jr., Choctaw, of Natchitoches, Louisiana. In 1984, I invited him to participate in a Woodland basketry symposium and also invited Martha Ross, Cherokee basket maker of North Carolina, who remained a lifelong friend. Claude initially seemed to be a vagabond, traveling and staying extended times with various people. I soon realized he was a dedicated researcher, giving his all to baskets and arts of the Woodlands, and was doing so in the face of obstacles that would deter most people. We began corresponding, and his multi-page letters provided generous information. I made a finger-woven sash for him and gained one of his beautiful cane baskets in exchange. That basket now resides with the National Museum of the American Indian, and my sash is at the Williamson Museum in Natchitoches, where all the fine things Claude collected went when he died too early. I also gave my letters from Claude to the museum, as did many other people (hardly anyone threw away his typed single-spaced, multi-page letters). Occasionally I still come across one, in an obscure file or pressed in a pertinent book, and Claude speaks to me again. When I moved back to Oklahoma around 1990, Claude advised me to look up Marshal Gettys at the Oklahoma Historical Society. Marshal was also dedicated to southeastern baskets, but from another perspective; he was a collector and a historian. He gained the ability, like Claude, to discern materials, methods and differentiations denoting one tribe's work from another. Marshal set me to this writing assignment, and he, too, left this world too soon. I was just learning about old baskets under his tutelage, and now, regrettably, I know just enough to be dangerous. The third man (number one in my life) is my husband, Jim Roaix, who enjoyed late-night sessions of basket making when Claude happened to visit us. Jim, of Maine, grew up using Micmac-produced ash baskets in potato field harvests, and he and Claude exchanged information and practiced each other's crafts into the wee hours, powered by coffee, pastries and an occasional potato baked in the microwave. Jim, who, like me, also enjoyed Marshal's vibrant personality and knowledge, continues to aid me with his own experience, a keen love of indigenous arts and his desire to assist me in my pursuit of capturing history.

The following individuals, roughly in order of contact, assisted this work by personally providing me with information and/or assistance affecting this published study: Mary Ellen Meredith, Tom Mooney, Mickel Yantz, Sharilyn Young, Christina Burke, Thomas Young, Patricia Nietfeld, Eric Singleton, Bob Pickering, Laura Bryant, Ollie Starr, Barbara Starr Scott, Bessie Russell, Anna Sixkiller, Jackie Coatney, Loretta Buffington, Billy Joe Sapp, Kathryn Roastingear, Linda Taylor, Clara Sue Kidwell, Mary Beth Nelson, John Timothy, Kimberley Gilliland, Terra Coons Fredrick, Matt Anderson, Dayna Lee, Luke Williams, Dana Talbert, Brenda Bradford, M. Anna Fariello, Catherine Sease, Roger Colten, Barbara Duncan, Jerry Catcher Thompson, Feather Smith, Stephanie Allen, Leta Jones, Matt Reed, Ketina Taylor, Shannon Fisher, Jacquelyn Reese, Ken Masters, Sarah H. Hill, Ted Foster, Ken Foster, Carolyn Chumwalooky, Jules-Marie Thornton, Mary Kay Henderson, Bobbie Gail Smith, Christy Sequichie, Rachel Henson, Nathan M. Gerth, Sheila Swearingen, Scott Swearingen, Steven Herrin, Rachel Mosman, Darcy Marlow, Phillip Viles, Vivian Cottrell, Mike Dart, Lisa Rutherford, Tennessee Loy and deepest thanks to Jeff Ross Davis, who served as a miracle worker with the photographs I amassed from a variety of sources. Apologies to all I overlooked.

INTRODUCTION

Basketry serves as an enduring thread of Cherokee culture in Oklahoma. Fifteen thousand peaceful and productive Cherokee people were forced to relocate to what is now Oklahoma 175 years ago.[1] Cherokee basket makers faced tremendous challenges during and following their removal to the West. Today, six to eight generations later, most Cherokee citizens living in the Cherokee Nation know the names of their antecedents who traveled the trail or moved west earlier or came later. Cherokee basket makers can be proud of their own tenacity and achievements. Their craft, due to basket maker persistence, represents one of the pinnacles of Cherokee cultural survival.

The market for Oklahoma Cherokee baskets is currently robust, but it has not always been so. Despite the fact that Cherokee basketry never disappeared in Oklahoma, the craft was long ignored in national and regional studies of indigenous basketry. The first major book regarding indigenous baskets, *Indian Basketry* by George Wharton James, was published in 1901 with over 250 illustrations, yet the only mention of Cherokee basketry is a short reference about use of dyes. Next, Otis Tufton Mason's two-volume 1904 *American Indian Basketry*, with 460 illustrations (none Cherokee) and more than five hundred pages, used only a paragraph to acknowledge the fineness of early Cherokee cane basketwork and ignored the continuation and evolution of the craft.

While Cherokee culture was studied by ethnographer James Mooney beginning in 1885 until his death in 1921,[2] Mooney said very little about

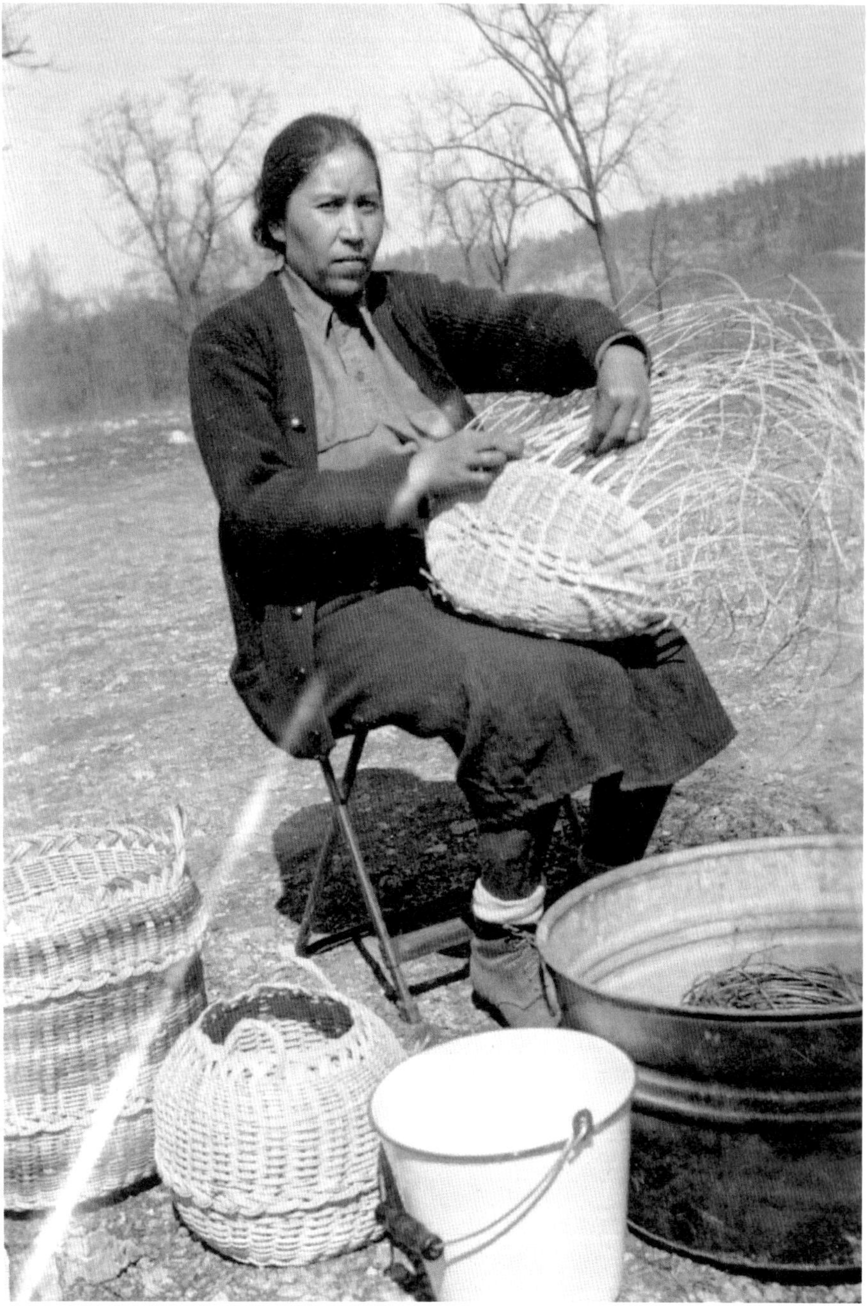

Eliza Proctor of Kenwood Community working on a buckbrush basket in 1941. *National Archives at Fort Worth.*

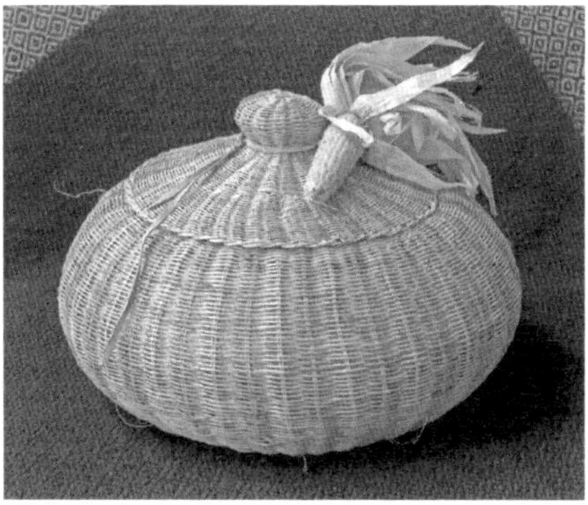

Lena Blackbird made this large buckbrush basket with knob-handled lid decorated with an ear of corn, now in a private collection. *Jeff Davis.*

Cherokee basketry even though one of his primary informants in North Carolina was basket maker Sally Terrapin (*Ayasta*). Mooney collected seven of her baskets, now at the Smithsonian's National Museum of Natural History, but he was more interested in what she knew about Cherokee legends.[3] Mooney reported that *Wadi-yahi*, "the last old woman who preserved the art of making double-walled baskets," died during an epidemic in 1897 in North Carolina.[4] Even though he proclaimed her to be "the last," the practice persisted. *Last of the Mohicans*, published by James Fenimore Cooper in 1826, convinced the public that the Mahicans were gone, but people and practices persist beyond obvious perception in the same way Oklahoma Cherokee basketry persisted. Mooney conducted research with Cherokee informants in both the East and the West, focusing his work on Cherokee history and belief systems as evidenced by legends and medicines. He did not record much about crafts, daily practices and routine activities or intergenerational or gender relationships.[5] Mooney's work did very little to further interest in the development and continuation of Cherokee material culture, including baskets.

Ethnologist Frank G. Speck's 1920 "Decorative Art and Basketry of the Cherokee," published as a *Bulletin of the Public Museum of the City of Milwaukee*, focused entirely on one museum's collection of North Carolina baskets, thus ignoring Oklahoma Cherokee basketry. Oklahoma Cherokee basket makers, meanwhile, were making workbaskets, sewing baskets, food-serving baskets and storage baskets, plus curio baskets. Oklahoma Cherokee basket makers were starving for attention and would continue to be overlooked in the decades ahead.

Grace Steele Woodward reported in her 1963 history book, *The Cherokees*, "Basket-making…apparently has not made headway in eastern Oklahoma. But why this is so the Cherokees themselves do not know."[6] Part of the problem stemmed from early Cherokee Nation efforts to isolate itself, requiring outsiders to have a permit to enter and warding off railroad incursions into the heartland. After 1907 statehood removed control from the Cherokee

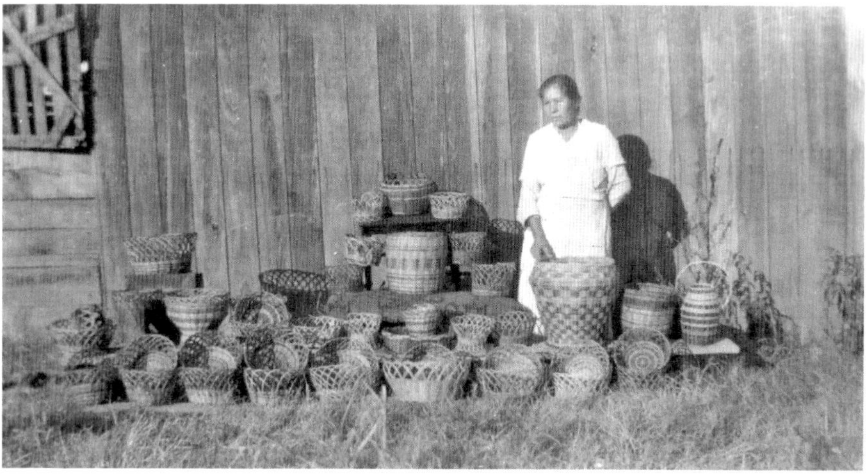

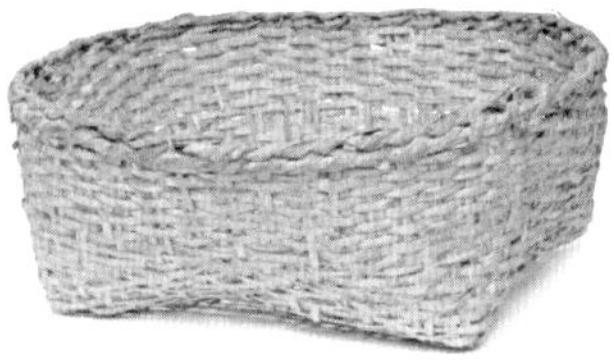

Above: Nannie Hogner's family was self-supporting due to basket-making perseverance. *Carl Albert Center Congressional Archives, University of Oklahoma.*

Left: This old hickory splint sifter, collected by Clark Field, was made around 1890 at Fort Gibson. *Philbrook Museum of Art.*

Nation, railroads extended their lines, but passenger service declined by the mid-twentieth century. Into the 1960s, rural Cherokee areas suffered from lack of paved roads, paucity of bridges and a dearth of telephone lines and electricity. It was hard to get the word out and equally hard for contacts to get in. Even today, the prevalence of low-water bridges (concrete pads imbedded into stream beds) leads to occasional closing of roads. Cellphone reception is spotty, GPS often cannot deliver a driver to remote locations and rutted country roads intimidate urbanites.

Basket makers, meanwhile, have long been engaged in an arduous effort to gain recognition and remuneration for their skills. To understand their struggle, one must first understand the heritage of Cherokee basket making and the historical events that split the Cherokee population, leaving one group to continue in the East and forcing a larger group of Cherokee citizens to obscurity in the West. The history of Oklahoma Cherokee basket making goes hand in hand with the history of Oklahoma Cherokee people.

Readers will find a list of known Oklahoma Cherokee basket makers born before 1930 at the end of this book, followed by references to collections totaling more than five hundred Oklahoma Cherokee baskets.

CHEROKEE BASKETRY BEGINS IN THE EAST

1700–1838

In the early mists of time, Cherokee artisans began producing beautiful and useful baskets and mats from harvested cane, split into long, pliable weaving staves. Dyes produced from bloodroot and nut hulls provided a tricolor palette of rusty red and brownish black along with the sallow hue of natural cane coating. By manipulating these complementary hues, various complex patterns were created by expert designers and crafters.

One of the earliest mentions of Cherokee baskets was published in 1714 by British government surveyor John Lawson, who wrote, "A great way up the Country, both Baskets and Mats are made of split Reed which are only the outward shining part of the Cane. Of these I have seen Mats, Baskets, and Dressing Boxes, very artificially done." Lawson meant the baskets he observed were the products of artisanal skill, and he also informs the reader that he knew that when cane was split, the shiny side he saw was the original outer covering of the plant.[7] Skilled cane basket makers were careful to place the cane splints so as to show the best side of the material.

Producing baskets with double walls is a Cherokee weaving tradition from time immemorial, and such baskets are made by the Cherokee and a few other tribes in North America.[8] Fine examples of early Cherokee baskets reside in the British Museum's Sloane Collection, having been obtained in 1725.[9] A description provided by South Carolina colonial governor Francis Nicholson, in an inventory regarding the baskets, says, "Strips of cane of two thicknesses are used in the weaving, thereby allowing different patterns

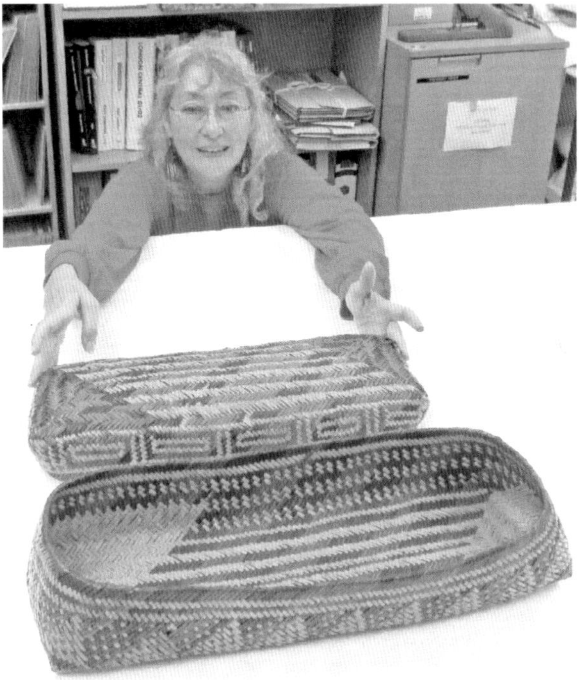

Leta Jones of the Oklahoma Native American Basketweavers Association visited the British Museum in London to view a circa 1725 Cherokee cane basket. *Bonnie Sharp.*

to be formed on the inside and outside. The two distinct parts of the basket are interwoven for a distance of some two inches from the edge."[10]

Nicholson's "two thicknesses" refers to the double walls of the particular basket, whereby one decorative tri-color pattern can occur inside the basket while a different pattern may appear on the outside wall of the basket. Accomplishing this feat is an incredible achievement when one considers the craftswoman was using long dyed weaving strips that would continue throughout the entire construction, moving only straight on their path with no "lane changes" occurring. The making of two different controlled images from the same splints that diverge and re-cross does not accidentally occur; the planning involves mathematical precision. Nicholson's explanation also describes how the two walls are united as the materials approach the bottom edge. The interweaving is hidden to all but the keenest of observers.

The final part of the cane double-weave process occurs after the bottom has received its second wall, whereupon the final ends of splints are worked into and under existing bottom splints upon reaching the far edge of the basket bottom. Excess lengths are snipped sharply off while the splint ends lie locked under protective covering splints.

A doubled wall provides added strength and weight, and since light hardly filters through the two layers of the walls, the basket pattern shows to its best dramatic advantage. Because cane is only flexible after it has been split, one side of a split cane weaver retains its natural glossy coating while the interior side is dull due to exposed inner pith. In the case of proficient basket makers, the pith side will be hidden inside the walls of the weaving.[11]

The process of developing intricate interwoven twilled patterns with dyed cane splits is complex. A design must be organized so the diagonally woven materials run as planned in color sets to the four sides, where the color sets converge exactly where the weaver needs them in order to produce the desired balanced design. If you start out with the wrong count or the wrong order of splints, the design elements will not come together as desired.

Shawna Morton Cain, a Cherokee National Living Treasure and Oklahoma Cherokee basket maker, explains, "If they're not divisible by twelve, your pattern won't work out. To do these designs you have to understand mathematics and you have to be able to divide and multiply….I always like to teach that with graph paper with kids because it shows that if you didn't have an understanding of higher math…you couldn't have been a basket weaver."[12]

Early Cherokee women routinely made arrays of large cane storage baskets, most often with fitted lids, which also could serve as trays. Women developed patterns and provisioned their homes with sturdy storage baskets of varying sizes, often nesting into one another in graduated sizes to save storage space between periods of use.[13] Not every Cherokee basket was double woven. Baskets were pervasive in early Cherokee life, being used

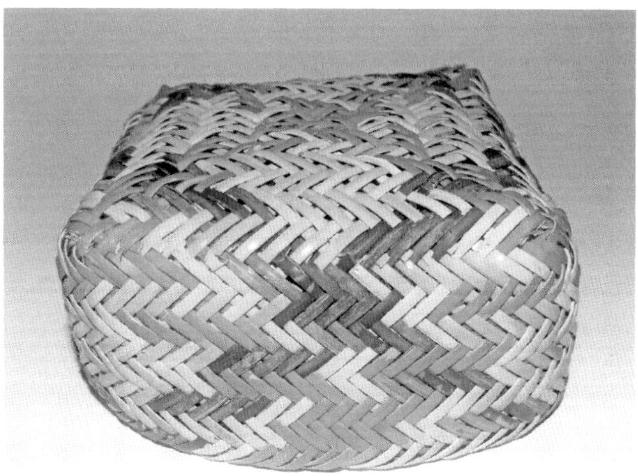

Snipped ends of cane splints are hidden at the bottom edge of a basket made by Charlotte Coats. *Jim Roaix.*

for ceremonial vessels, as food processing implements, as appurtenances in every home and village and valued as popular bartering items. Baskets appear in legends and were used in a once-popular Cherokee dice game, with beans serving as two-sided dice marked on one side and tossed from, and caught in, a basket.[14]

Soon after Europeans arrived, trade goods began to replace traditional household items and clothing, yet wooden trunks and boxes and kegs did not quickly replace Cherokee basketry. In fact, the beautiful baskets themselves became part of the colonial trade system. John Adair, Indian agent, said in 1775 that Cherokee baskets had been "highly esteemed...for domestic usefulness, beauty, and skillful variety" and had drawn a handsome price from admiring colonists.[15] Keen to sell and trade baskets, Cherokee basket makers were willing to adapt their work to buyers' needs.

The establishment of the United States as a liberated and new nation led to an increase of immigrant populations hungry for land. Soon various foreign-born nationals became American frontiersmen seeking real estate and opportunity. These families initially had little interest in procuring decorative items. They called on their state governments to remove Cherokee people and other large and small tribal groups from the eastern states. Following the Louisiana Purchase, there was a place to resettle the indigenous people: a big amorphous land west of the Mississippi, already occupied by its own resident American Indians, and therefore newly titled Indian Territory. As time passed, the designation of Indian Territory referred to ever-smaller swaths of land and lastly referred to just the eastern side of Oklahoma.

As early as 1792, many Cherokee citizens began escaping growing tensions in the East by moving west of the Mississippi River to what is now Missouri and then on to what is now northwest Arkansas in 1811. The first Cherokees in the West eventually numbered about four thousand people and gained the name Old Settlers.[16] Old Settler Cherokee women would have studied their new environment and made baskets based on their discoveries and needs.

Susan C. Power's *Art of the Cherokee* discusses two unusual baskets attributed to Cherokee Margaret Scott Vann, associated with the Moravian mission to the Cherokee called Springplace, located in northwest Georgia.[17] These baskets are perhaps the earliest examples of Cherokee "root runner" baskets. The translated and recently published *Records of the Moravians Among the Cherokee* includes a letter of September 1810 reporting that Cherokee convert Margaret Scott Vann was sending six baskets to the Salem, North Carolina Moravian headquarters with a request that the baskets be given to specific individuals. The letter further notes that some of the baskets were

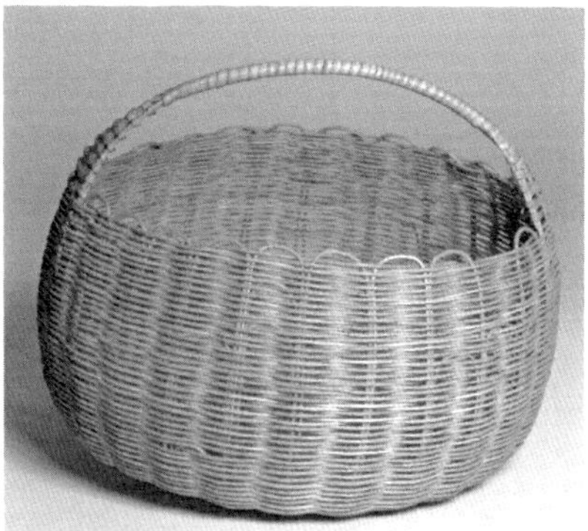

A Cherokee weaver in Georgia near Springplace Moravian mission made root runner baskets before Removal. *Yale Peabody Museum.*

obtained by Vann through trade: "The remaining three, together with some others which she is sending to Br. and Sr. Kramsch [were] got by trading beads of coral which were sent to her by a friend in Newark."[18]

The writer also noted that the "baskets have nothing special to recommend themselves except that they are made by Indian hands."[19] Sarah H. Hill noted in her study "Weaving History: Cherokee Baskets from the Springplace Mission," published in the *William and Mary Quarterly*, that Margaret Vann periodically sent Cherokee baskets to friends of Springplace.[20] We learn by the September 1810 entry that Margaret Vann did not make the baskets, or at least had not made all of them.

Four baskets in the collections of the Yale Peabody Museum of Anthropology in New Haven, Connecticut, were donated by the Moravian Historical Society.[21] Two are cane baskets, typical of Cherokee baskets of the era, but the other two are made of "root-runner."[22] Power and Hill both reported the basketry material to be absent of knots or nodules such as found on other familiar root runner materials.[23] Yale Peabody's senior conservator, Catherine Sease, provided this author with a close-up photograph capturing the appearance of knots/nodules seen at intervals on the weaving material of one of the baskets. If the material were determined to be honeysuckle, it would prove earlier use of that material than currently believed; if it were, on the other hand, noted to be buckbrush, it would prove the use of that particular material in the Southeast, confounding current belief that it had never been used in the Southeast. Only a cell sample of the plant material can provide certainty of the actual plant identity. However, these baskets, if donor information is correct, serve to prove pre-Removal use of root runners, establishing a link of tradition for Oklahoma Cherokee root runner basketry. Additionally, knowing Vann obtained many of her gifted baskets through trade suggests new forms such as sewing baskets and trinket baskets sprung from early Cherokee adaptations to market possibilities. While it is possible mission personnel may have influenced use of root runners, nothing provides that implication in the recently translated journals and letters

(Moravians wrote and spoke an old form of German). The mission journals are noted for their attention to detail.

Removal plans enacted in 1838 intended to remove all Cherokees from their ancient Appalachian homeland. However, a remnant Cherokee group managed to escape removal and eventually acquired a land base, titled Qualla Boundary, in western North Carolina. This group is now federally recognized as the Eastern Band of Cherokee Indians (EBCI). When an area of the Smoky Mountains later became the most visited United States National Park, founded in 1934, the Cherokee of North Carolina found themselves straddling the southern entryway to the park. Tourist industry businesses flocked to the area, leasing land from the local Cherokee government in order to service visitors with lodging, food and tourist attractions.[24]

The Eastern Cherokee wisely established their own arts and crafts cooperative in 1946, followed by their successful Museum of the Cherokee Indian. The craft cooperative established unwavering quality control and set fair prices, launching North Carolina Cherokee basketry as a successful enterprise, making it possible for several talented, hardworking Cherokee people in the area to make a living from traditional craft skills.[25]

In addition to beautifully made traditional cane baskets, white oak baskets and honeysuckle runner baskets eventually became popular and are produced today by Eastern Cherokee basket makers. Cane is the more difficult material to work with, making those baskets the priciest. Oak is a bit easier to work and oak trees are plentiful, so large oak baskets can be produced at reasonable prices. Oak baskets were often made for new uses such as handled gathering baskets and purse baskets, as well as handsome wastebaskets. Honeysuckle proved ideal for smaller items, sold at lesser cost and in great numbers as souvenir gift items. Eastern Cherokee baskets became the penultimate Cherokee basketry in the minds of collectors and curators, and ensuing books and exhibitions tended to focus on baskets from Qualla Boundary, while ignoring Oklahoma Cherokee baskets.

Further information about North Carolina basketry can be found in the 1991 *Studies in Cherokee Basketry* by Betty J. Duggan and Brett H. Riggs (which includes a reprint of Frank G. Speck's "Decorative Art and Basketry of the Cherokee"), Sarah H. Hill's 1997 *Weaving New Worlds: Southeastern Cherokee Women and Their Basketry* and *Cherokee Basketry: From the Hands of our Elders* by M. Anna Fariello, published by The History Press in 2009.

NEW BEGINNINGS IN THE WEST

1839

Ultimately, most Cherokee citizens (about fifteen thousand in number) were forcibly removed in groups to the West in 1838–39.[26] Initially, people were rounded up by soldiers and not allowed to gather possessions.[27] Later, as authorities realized they were not prepared to sufficiently care for the detainees, they allowed people to retrieve or bring from their homes items useful in the impoundments. Often items were later lost or abandoned along the journey at flooded river crossings, sunk on failed barges or left on the side of the road alongside broken wagons. My own ancestors found it necessary, before the final leg of their pre-Removal journey, to store their possessions in an Arkansas barn, but when they returned to retrieve items, everything worthwhile had been pillaged.[28]

What sorts of baskets had people left behind? Interestingly, records relating to Removal provide information that otherwise would not have been recorded. The United States agreed to the reimbursement of Cherokee families for losses, and those claims tell us what items existed at that time in Cherokee households.

Cherokee citizen John Vann, for instance, declared his Removal losses in a document known as a "spoliation" claim. In addition to lost livestock and furniture, Vann calculated the loss of twenty-nine baskets valued at a total of $20.50, which equates to over $400.00 today.[29] Vann listed more than a dozen cane baskets, including three that were specifically described as double-woven baskets, along with six sifters, four fanners and four "back baskets" of unnoted materials.[30]

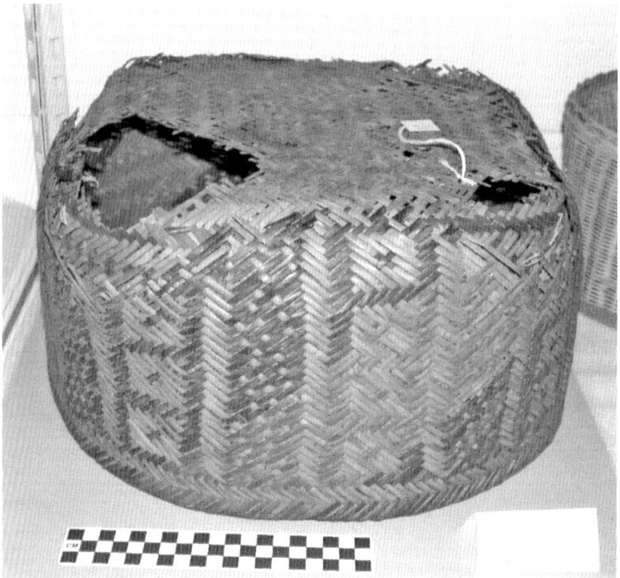

This old cane basket survived the Removal trip to be collected by historian Alice Marriott, who donated it to the University of Oklahoma in 1956. *Sam Noble Museum of Natural History.*

It would be remiss not to mention that John Vann, a Cherokee citizen, was among a few wealthy Cherokees who owned a number of black slaves.[31] While his losses would not be a typical example, his situation serves to remind us of other factors to consider. Recent studies of pottery in colonial America find a rough pottery called "colonoware," which is noted to exhibit both American Indian and African influences. Examples of this pottery have been found not only in European-American settlements but also in southeastern American Indian villages.[32]

In reality, no culture is an island. American Indians would, at times, adopt foreign methods affecting old traditions. It is not known who made John Vann's baskets, nor is it known if slaves held by Cherokee families were instructed to produce baskets for households only in the Cherokee manner. At this time, there is no documented evidence of Cherokee basketry traditions having been influenced by African traditions, but there have been active discussions about other possible influences, such as the possibility of the use of materials like oak or root runners as derivative of white influence, about handles having been introduced after white contact and about particular basket shapes or uses being influenced by white practices. With certainty, as the earliest Cherokee basket makers refined their craft they were influenced by their tribal neighbors and in turn influenced those neighbors and later were influenced by newcomers to the ancient homeland. Innovation and borrowing are admirable human traits necessary for survival in challenging times.

A study of all spoliation claims finds Cherokee families in the East had generally owned from two to twenty baskets. Basket types listed on the claims included fanners (for winnowing), riddles or riddlers (large-gauge sieves), small-gauge sifters, bread trays, lidded storage baskets and pack baskets. Many of the baskets were noted as being made of canes, while others lacked material references.[33]

Informative narratives regarding not only baskets but life in general, as remembered by early settlers of Oklahoma, are found in the 1937 Indian-Pioneer Papers of the Western History Collections at the University of Oklahoma in Norman and at the Research and Archives Division of the Oklahoma Historical Society in Oklahoma City. The interviews were collected during the Great Depression as a Works Progress Administration (WPA) project whereby older individuals expressed their memories and sometimes relayed information they had heard from predecessors. These interviews have provided a great resource for today's area historians. Several of the interviewees mentioned Cherokee baskets. Most of their descriptions were of workbaskets, single-walled baskets of cane or wood.

For instance, Lucinda Hickey, born in Stilwell in 1854, described the preparation of hominy, noting two kinds of baskets for sifting the pestle-pounded hominy corn: "It was…put into a cane basket with the bottom made of open work and sifted through to remove finer husks from the corn. It was then put into a closer woven basket and fanned…to take the bran from the first hominy. This was called a fanner."[34]

Rachel Gann Dodge, whose grandmother Aggie Silk endured the Trail of Tears (1838–39), described a riddle basket: "Take cane and cut it in long strips, weave a basket with square holes in the bottom but close sides. Use it like a sieve…put the corn that has been beaten in the mortar with the pestle, in the riddle and shake it over a pan. The grits will stay in the riddle and the flour will fall in the pan."[35] Sue Ann Emerson, Cherokee, recorded her grandfather's memory of watching Cherokee girls in the late 1890s using a cane riddle basket to scoop up buckeye-stunned fish from a stream.[36]

Sieves (including sifters and riddlers) would be made of different spacing according to purpose, and a home would likely have an array of such baskets. A basket at the Oklahoma Historical Society is woven loosely at the center of the bottom, but the openings were increasingly tightened as it progressed toward the walls. This would allow sifting into a bowl.

Dodge provided further information: "The fanning pan is made exactly like the riddle, except it is closely woven to keep the flour in. It takes skill to use the fanning pan correctly. They shake the pan to get the flour in the

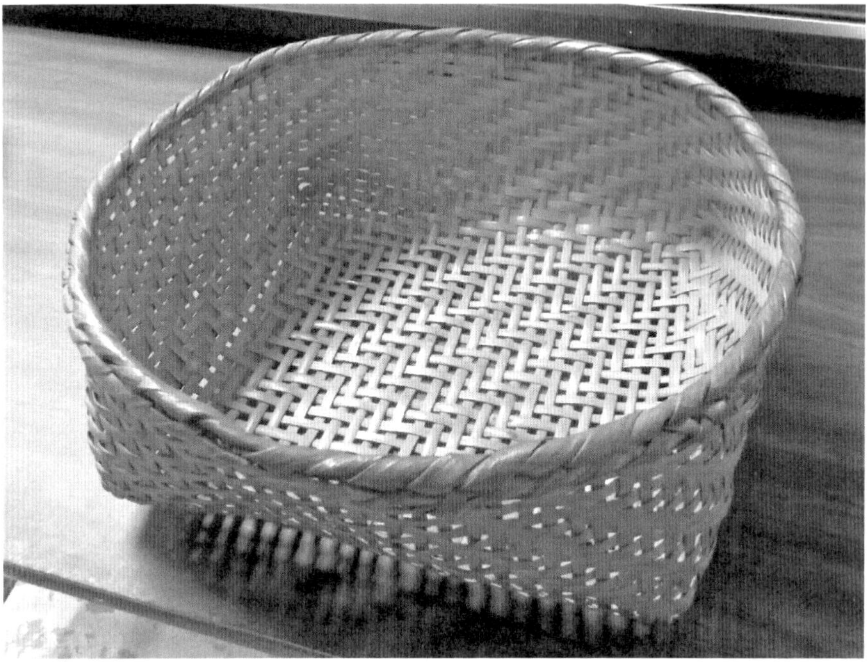

The Snell family of Jay used their "kenuche basket" for generations to make a traditional recipe of pounded and sifted hickory nuts formed into balls. *Jim Roaix.*

bottom of the pan with the grits on top, then they give it a little jerk and the grits jump over the edge of the fanning pan into another that is setting on the table."[37]

Some fanning baskets, however, were shaped very differently from the riddle basket. Oklahoma historian Muriel Wright describes another form: "The fanner is woven of split cane in the shape of a shovel about thirty inches long, with one end open and flat; the other end, with the edges rolled up about four inches forms a pocket-like receptacle. The fanner is held in the hands and shaken to toss the broken pieces of grain so that the husks gather at the front, open end and the broken kernels roll back into the pocket-like receptacle."[38]

Arlie Reeves, of Webbers Falls, had been orphaned and went through the fourth grade at the orphanage in Salina. Her grandfather was known as Buzzard Flopper, and she was able to do all the traditional crafts and live self-sufficiently in her elder years. She had been born in 1867 and mentioned making baskets from hickory bark (inner bark strips), as well as buckbrush.[39]

Another report noted, "Ladles were made by taking a small hickory limb and bend it to make a circle or hoop. Take pieces of tender young cane stripping the outside of it into fine strings and weave like a chair bottom, leaving a large mesh."[40]

Washing dug-up potatoes called for oak or hickory workbaskets. Potatoes would be rolled back and forth in a large-gauge sifter-bottomed basket dunked in water, causing the potatoes to get an effective scouring from the edges of the rough wood splints.[41]

Cherokee basket makers adopted a lashed rim for their workbaskets, applying a pliant rod to the basket edge. It was not the prettiest rim, but it probably felt substantial and secure to the user of the basket. Choctaw basket makers preferred a rolled rim as well as rolled handles, or sometimes braided rims and handles.[42]

These are the sorts of baskets needed in every home, and there is no doubt that Cherokee women arriving in Indian Territory would at the first opportunity begin producing an array of workday baskets.

HISTORICAL BASKETS WITH TIES TO EAST AND WEST

A few old Cherokee baskets have been noted as survivors of the Trail of Tears. One such basket is a privately owned sifter made of wood material and pictured in the book *The Cherokee Trail of Tears*.[43] It has appeared in two exhibitions at the Cherokee Heritage Center near Tahlequah, the capital city of the Oklahoma Cherokee.

Another Trail of Tears traveler is a cane storage basket collected by Alice Marriott, who had worked with Cherokee basket makers while managing a Works Progress Administration project in Oklahoma. As a trained and noted historian, she is likely to have critically assessed historical information regarding the basket. The basket, not in pristine condition, was gifted in 1956 to the University of Oklahoma and is now at the Sam Noble Oklahoma Museum of Natural History in Norman. It is seven inches tall, with a lid, and is fifteen inches in diameter, woven in a pattern called Birds Eye.[44]

A published caption in the 1964 booklet *The Art and the Romance of Indian Basketry*, authored by collector Clark Field, about an old basket has been found to be suspect. On page twenty-five of Field's study, a cane-woven quiver is noted as having been brought by a specific historic person to Oklahoma before 1860. However, Philbrook Museum's accession records state that the quiver was actually made in the 1940s by a North Carolina Cherokee craftsman at the request of an ethnologist, who then sold the piece to Field, where it became part of the Philbrook Collection in Tulsa.[45] It is not known how the misattribution occurred in the publication. Perhaps Field had at one time possessed an early basket quiver and confused the two when

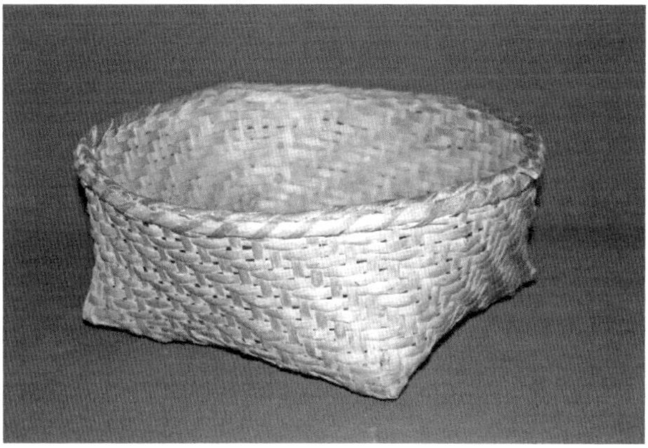

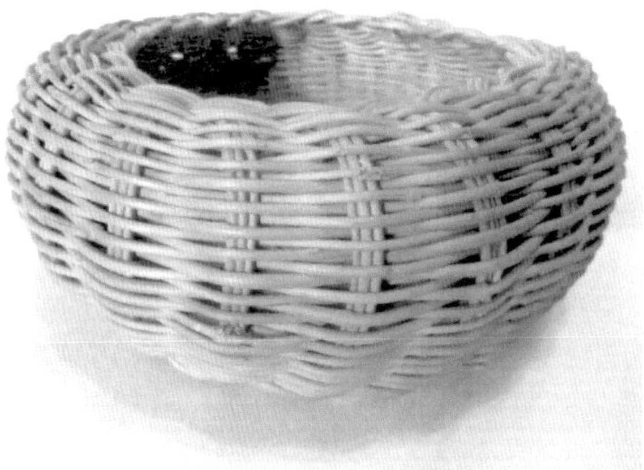

Top: This wood basket, privately owned, was exhibited at the Cherokee Heritage Center as a Trail of Tears basket. *Cherokee National Historical Society.*

Left: This stout buckbrush basket exemplifies early forms of runner baskets similar to the Yale Peabody runner baskets and Bacone College's early buckbrush basket. *Jim Roaix.*

preparing captions. His daughter Dorothy did provide an interview in 1937 discussing her father's basket collection before it was given to Philbrook, and she referred to a Cherokee split cane basket brought with Removal,[46] but Philbrook has no such basket in its Field Collection. Perhaps Field had traded the basket or later questioned the validity of its story.

Another mystery-inducing basket is shown in *Cherokee*, a 2002 photography book by David Fitzgerald authored by Robert Conley, where a caption notes, "Old Cherokee basket c. 1838. The basket is said to have come over the Trail of Tears."[47] Accession records for the basket at Bacone College in Muskogee cite the basket as having belonged to the donor's great-great-grandmother, but the ancestor's name or birthdate is not noted, and the donor provided no contact information or family history.[48] It has a lid and once had a handle; it is exceptionally clean and unworn and might have been little used and kept covered in a dark closet during most of its existence. The double-woven stout sewing basket is made of buckbrush, and Cherokee basketry authorities have said buckbrush was not used in the East,[49] making the tale of arriving via the Trail of Tears questionable.

However, if the basketry material of the Yale Peabody Museum's early runner baskets made by Georgia Cherokees were to be identified as buckbrush, the information would change long-held assertions that buckbrush was never used in the East, even though it was available in the Southeast.[50] If the material were determined to be honeysuckle, it would prove earlier use of that material than currently believed. Perhaps the Bacone basket cannot summarily be denied a history as provided by its donor. But currently, the older Peabody basket cannot qualify the status of the younger Bacone basket. The older Peabody basket does, however, tell us that Cherokee runner baskets were not unknown in the old homeland before Removal.

CHEROKEE BASKETRY EVOLUTION IN THE WEST

1840–1900

Upon arrival in Indian Territory, bereft of adequate household items, the vast majority of Cherokee women would have immediately set to work producing a needed array of workbaskets.[51] A small number of households maintained a workforce of slaves, so it cannot be said that all Cherokee women began producing baskets, but most would have found it necessary to do so.

External and internal political strife occurring before and during the Removal process plagued the transplanted Cherokees, much of it with high costs to individuals. There was an urgency to reestablish Cherokee government functions and reunite the Old Settlers with the new arrivees, but equally important to individuals was the building of cabins, barns and fences and clearing of fields and pastureland. Most women were faced with endless tasks of tending sick and weakened families, feeding them, sewing and mending worn-out clothing, weaving new cloth and making quilts, planting household gardens, cooking and foraging in unfamiliar Ozark woodlands or grasslands for plants suitable for food, medicine and craft materials.

Arriving in the West, Cherokee basket makers found a different environment—familiar, but definitely *not* the same they had experienced in the southern Appalachians. Cherokee Nation territory in Oklahoma consists of fourteen counties in the northeastern corner of the state

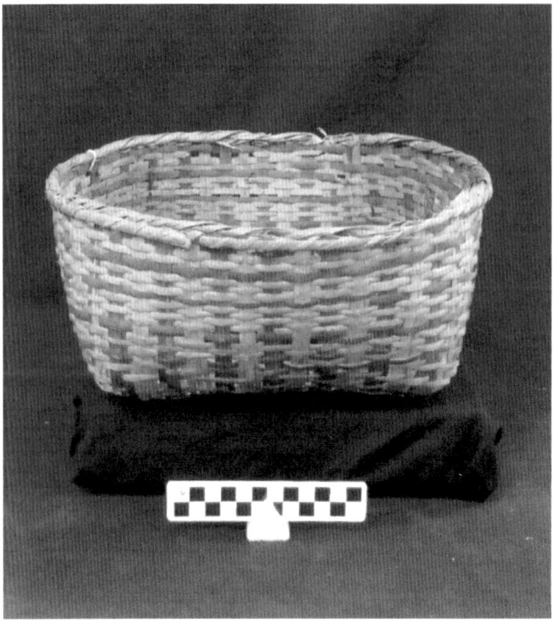

This cane basket, noted as seventy-five years old in 1920, was collected from Letitia Chamberlin of Vinita. *Oklahoma Historical Society.*

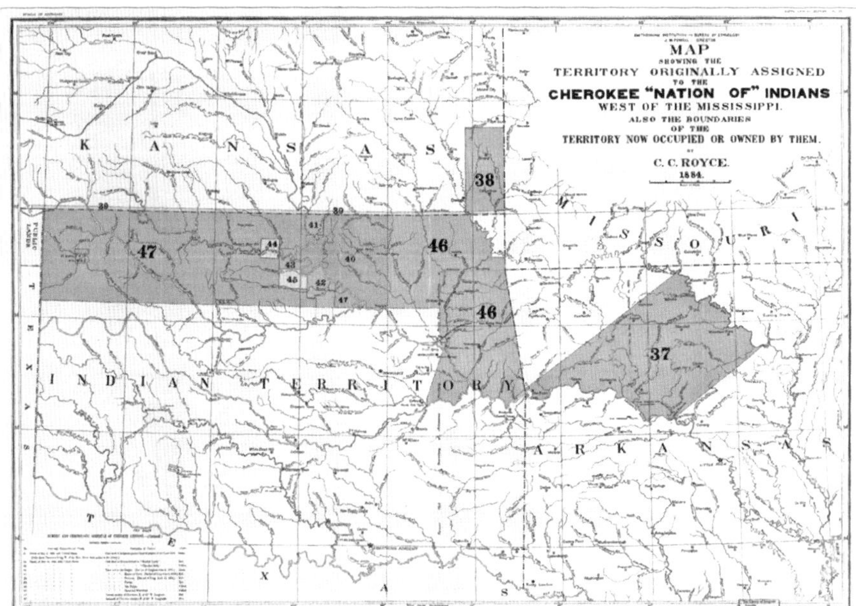

The Cherokee Nation once had more land than its current jurisdiction in northeastern Oklahoma, now the paired #46 portions of this 1884 map. *Library of Congress, Geography and Map Division.*

(abutting Arkansas, Kansas and Missouri). There are four eco-regions: Central Irregular Plains (northwest), Ozark Highlands (northeast), Boston Mountains (southeast) and the Arkansas River Valley running through the southern portion of the Cherokee Nation.[52]

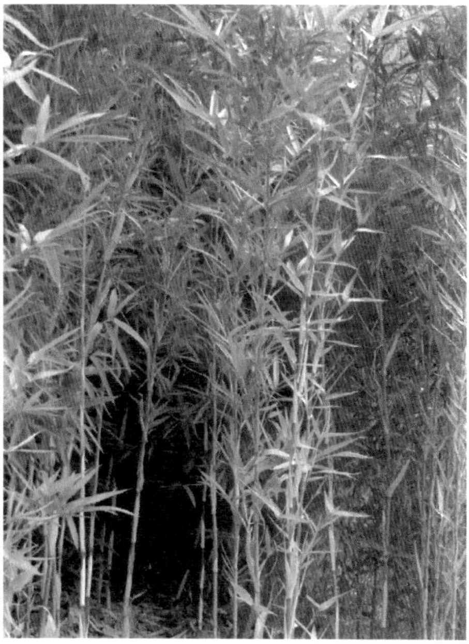

A stand of river cane is maintained by the Cherokee Nation in an indigenous plants and garden area. *Jim Roaix.*

Clark Field, an early basket collector, reported cane was not found in the Spavinaw hills in the north (nor would there have been much of it on the Plains grasslands to the west), but he noted cane to be plentiful in the Gore and Webbers Falls vicinity in the Arkansas River Valley at the southern boundaries, and it also occurred in the middle section of the Cherokee Nation, although not as abundantly as in the southern area.[53]

Plant qualities and the gathering seasons in the new territory differed from those of southern Appalachian forests.[54] Cane in the new land presented different characteristics due to hotter, drier climate and variations in soil. Rose Drake, a contemporary Cherokee woman weaving cane baskets in old patterns, described the process of cane preparation as she peeled fibrous material from inner parts of quartered cane stalks, popping the material away from each cane joint: "It has to be flexible, so you have to thin it. The first time I really worked with it, they had us bandage our fingers with athletic tape. With that silica, it gives you really bad paper cuts."[55]

Cane, hickory, oak, ash and willow would have been used, when possible, for replenishing the stock of much-needed household workbaskets.[56] "Hickory bark is also used to bind down the rim-hoops of practically all baskets," noted Carolyn Thomas Foreman.[57] Gatherers would have assessed their best options as they noted pliability, thickness, length, height and density of materials. As they used the local materials, they would have learned more about their workability, and as they used the baskets they made, they would learn still more about durability of the new materials. They would begin to

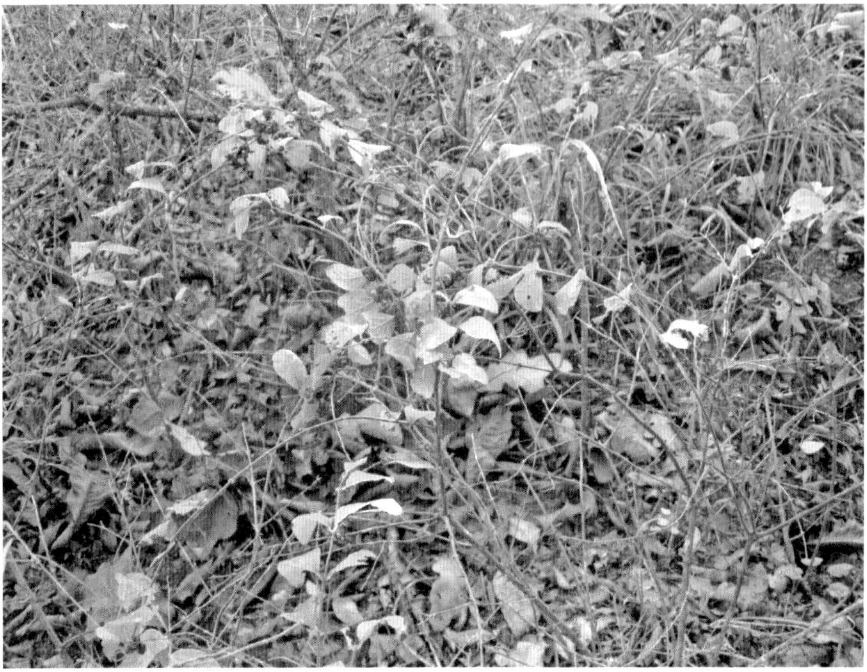

Buckbrush, also known as coralberry, has long roots at ground surface used for basket weaving. *Cherokee Nation.*

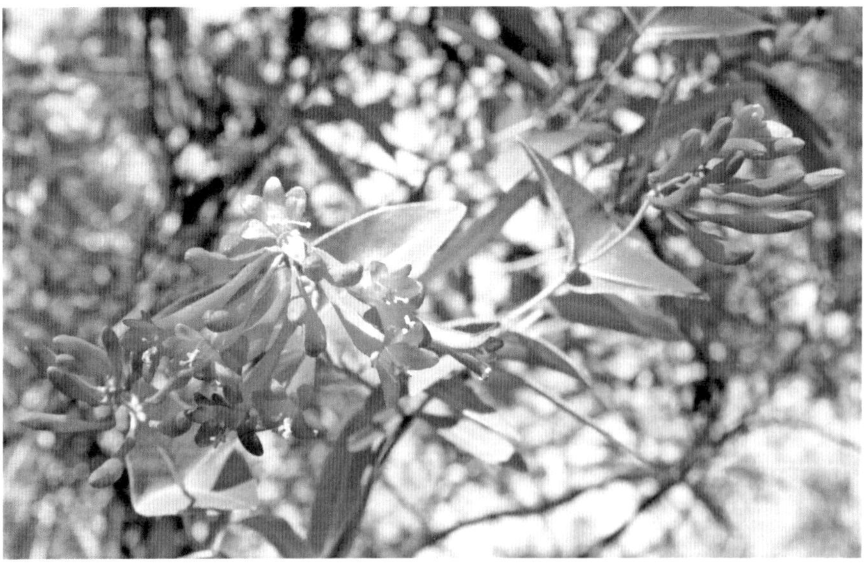

Indigenous honeysuckle varieties like this can be used for basketry, but the common invasive Japanese honeysuckle is widely used due to length and strength. *Amy Buthod.*

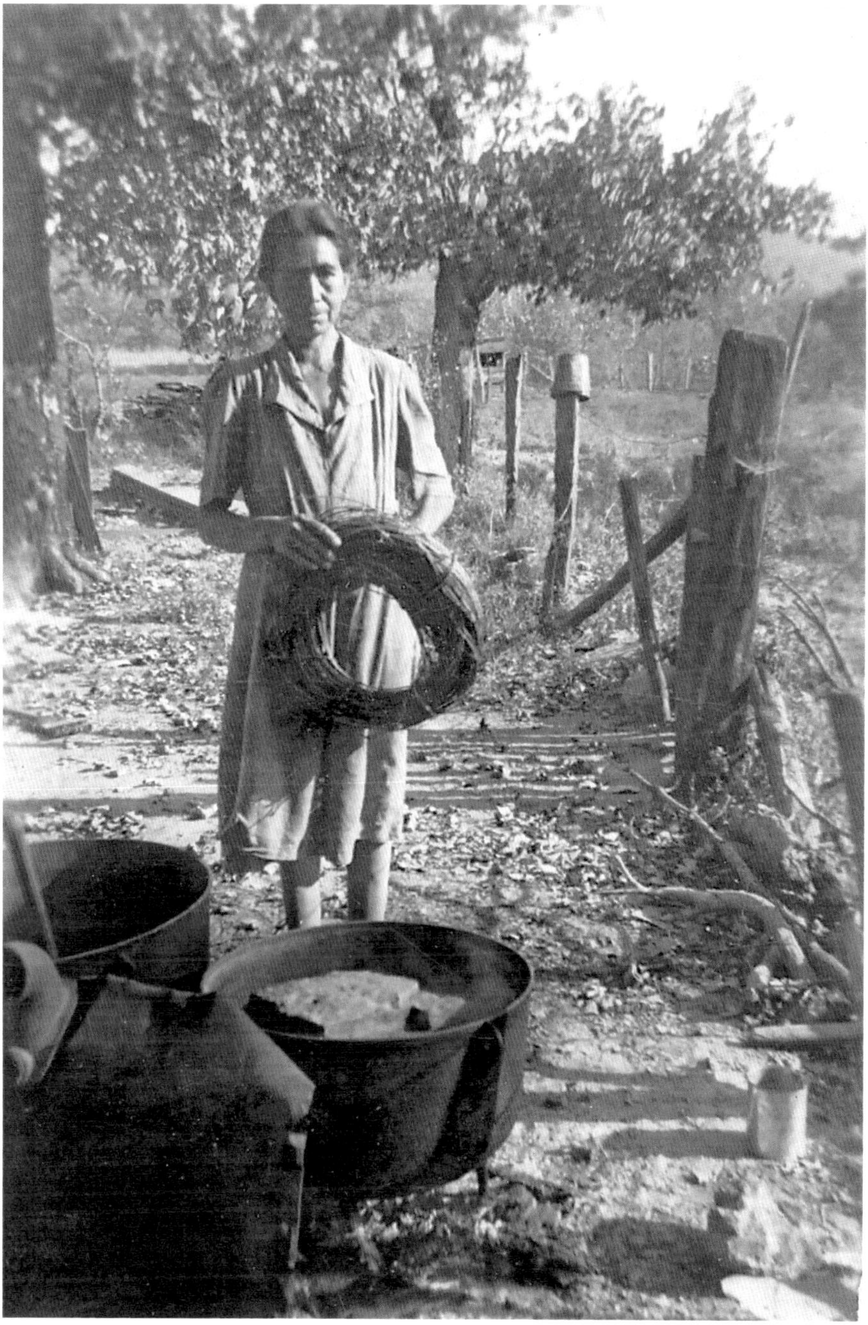

Lydia Adair prepares to boil a buckbrush coil in 1944. Boiling softens the bark of the root for easy removal. *National Archives at Fort Worth.*

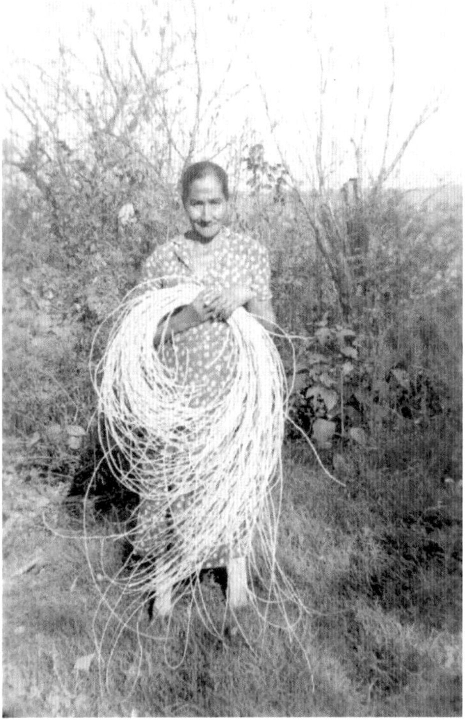

Annie Jones is seen here with harvested and prepared buckbrush root runners, ready for dye baths. *National Archives at Fort Worth.*

steer away from some materials due to disappointments, and they would continue to try new, previously unused materials.

Ultimately, Indian Territory Cherokee basket makers largely focused on a plant material highly suitable for producing double-woven baskets, although the material was very different from cane. The long roots of buckbrush, *Symphoricarpos orbiculatus*, run for extended distances just underneath the surface of the ground and are usually collected in the fall, dried for a few weeks in coils and then boiled to loosen the root bark,[58] which is removed by wiping the still-wet runners with a damp cloth or by wearing and using moistened cloth gloves to swipe off the coating, as seen in the video *Cherokee Basket Maker*.[59] Plentiful in the Ozarks, the bush prefers post oak forests.[60] The material is sufficiently strong, and the dried runners regain pliability after being placed in water. The plant itself is a bush standing two to four feet tall and is also known as coral berry, Indian currant, birds-eye bush or devil's shoestring because the roots are often tripped over.[61]

"The longest runners are found near the base of the plant and many are from 12 to 20 feet long. They are then wound together and tied in a roll and placed in a pot of water to boil for 3 to 4 hours, or until the bark will slip off easily."[62]

"It is said that the buckbrush is not a true medium of Indian use, that it should be accredited to the Ozark Hill folks," reported a *Tulsa World* feature article that added, "It is the only material they can obtain in abundance."[63] However, we know from the Yale Peabody Museum's 1810 runner basket that this form of basketry was not unknown to the Cherokee before moving west.

Further, the heritage of "Ozark Hill folks" had likely been influenced and schooled by Cherokee Old Settlers who escaped the tensions in the brash new United States by moving outside its borders and arriving in northwest Arkansas in the early nineteenth century prior to Removal and ultimately reconnected with the main body of Western Cherokees after the Trail of Tears.[64] Undoubtedly, Old Settler Cherokee women produced baskets during those earliest days in the West and developed a familiarity with the plants of the area. Basket collector Clark Field ascertained through discussion with Oklahoma Cherokee basket makers that Cherokee buckbrush baskets were made as early as 1850.[65] Buckbrush use by Old Settler Cherokees possibly occurred earlier.

Buckbrush is woven in a form known as wickerwork, whereby there are designated spokes or ribs forming the skeleton of the basket while another piece serves as filler, weaving over and under the ribs, circling around the basket, with a new runner piece inserted as the previous begins to diminish in length. Changes in basket texture can be accomplished by changing the ratio from one-over-one to one-over-two, two-over-two, one-over-three or other combinations.[66] The resulting texture can become a design element when ratios are changed during the weaving. And, of course, dyed pieces can produce bands or blocks of color.

Buckbrush runners prove highly suitable for weaving double-wall baskets, a traditional Cherokee basketry style relying on flexible weaving material. To double weave round runners, you start with a crisscross of pairs of moistened runners, all to serve as ribs. They are bound together by taking a long moist runner and weaving it over and under around the crisscrossed pieces, ultimately separating them into pairs or even singles as the basket grows in dimension. Most basket makers insert an added rib, or a paired set, to create an uneven number of rib sets and continue weaving the long runner over and under the ribs. This will make a flat bottom, like a saucer. The weaving is called wickerwork. After the bottom of the basket has reached the desired dimension, the ribs of the moistened weaving materials are turned upward, and the weaving continues on, climbing upward to make the interior sidewalls as it goes. Before a working runner is depleted, it is overlapped with one end of a newly added long runner. At the desired height of the basket, the moist weaving materials are turned aside and outward, forming a top basket rim of arches. The weaving continues through the now down-bent ribs alongside the original wall (at this point, the basket maker usually turns the basket upside down for easier manipulation). The weaving moves along the outside of the first

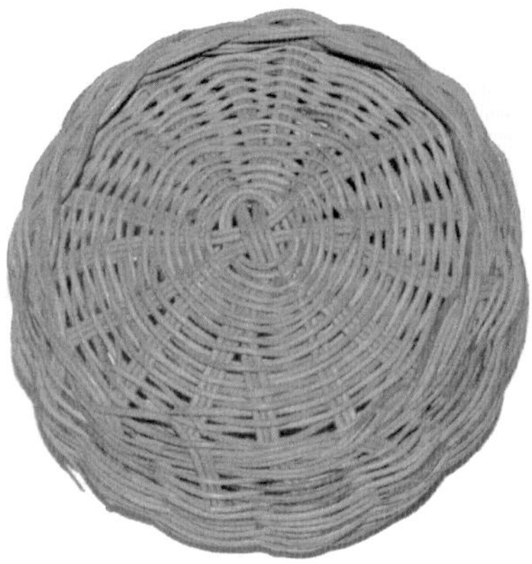

Root runner baskets start at the basket bottom with two groups of prepared runners placed at right angles, one atop the other. *Jim Roaix.*

wall, working toward the bottom of the basket, thus creating a doubled wall. Runner baskets usually are finished by manipulating the runners into an intertwined decorative platform at the outer edge of the basket bottom, or at a halfway point under the basket, where a pedestal is created by tight loops with the excess of the runner ends being snipped off, leaving a short remainder of the end of the runner to be inserted and hidden beneath a neighboring runner.

Basket styles changed not only due to new materials in a new location but also due to inevitable modernization pressures from outside sources, as well as due to innovations occurring from inside the culture of basket makers. The increasing establishment of gristmills by Cherokee proprietors in Indian Territory reduced the need for grain-processing workbaskets, and the inventories of Cherokee-managed general stores included wire sieves, metal colanders and lidded tin containers, all serving to replace utilitarian baskets.

Further, Cherokee leaders in Indian Territory developed a national Cherokee educational system in 1846 based on New England school practices and eventually included two schools of higher learning called seminaries, one for Cherokee men and another for women. Traditional Cherokee arts and cultural studies were not included in the coursework.[67] The students were being prepared to succeed in a white-controlled world that threatened to swallow them if they were not competitive.

The U.S. Civil War turned into a Cherokee civil war, closing their schools, scorching Indian Territory settlements and houses along major roadways and scattering refugees north to Kansas and south to Texas. Many baskets turned to ashes as homes were burned, adding to the gaps in the material record of basket history in the West. The war ended, leaving the Cherokee economy devastated, while families went uncompensated for losses of crops, livestock, buildings and furnishings. Indian Territory Cherokee cropland and pastures were choked with vines, bushes and saplings. The Cherokee people had to rise again (one reason the classical phoenix rising from the flames has become such a salient symbol for the Cherokee, serving as the name and logo of the Cherokee Nation *Phoenix* newspaper).

Importantly, in remote Indian Territory communities, old ways continued. Subsistence living (hunting, trapping, foraging, gardening and raising personal livestock) allowed families to survive without formal employment and was based on people making their own household goods. Women in those families continued making baskets for their own extended family use, passed on basket-making knowledge to their offspring and sold baskets—if anyone asked for one—or traded them for necessities.

The Cherokee Agricultural Society held the first fair in Indian Territory in 1845, but twenty-five years passed before a second fair occurred in 1870, sponsored by the Cherokee Farmers' Club. It was said to exhibit "articles of home manufacture" and was repeated the next year.[68] In 1875, the Indian International Fair Association was formed in Muskogee, with Joshua Ross, Cherokee, serving as secretary for the ongoing annual event. There was a judging category for the "best woven basket," along with other American Indian crafts.[69] In 1876, the Cherokee National Council formed a Fair and Agricultural Association and held its own event at Fort Gibson.[70] Fairs continued to spread as communities grew, and Muskogee and Tulsa, each just barely outside Cherokee territory, later began offering "state" fairs. The competitions and display areas were opportunities to gain notice for basketry skills as well as to sell baskets.

In the late nineteenth century, Indian Territory Cherokee basketwork transitioned from traditional work-related objects to Victorian-era-inspired decorative work with sweeping arches and fanciful curlicues. Cherokee basket makers responded to a growing market for pretty work by making items such as vases, cradles, bridal baskets, fruit baskets, bread trays, wall baskets, shopping baskets, picnic baskets, clothes hampers and magazine holders, as well as animal shapes.[71] Buckbrush proved ideal for these new forms due to flexibility in looping and turning without breaking or cracking when adequately moistened. These fancy baskets were items to be sold to affluent people and were rarely retained in basket makers' homes, leaving most descendants of early basket makers without heirloom examples of family works.[72] Luckily, for some descendants, early baskets survive in area museums, although too often such old baskets were made by someone whose identity went unrecorded.

Traditional dyes for enhancing baskets were initially derived from various indigenous plants, creating a muted palette of harmonious complementary colors. Bloodroot provides orangey-red, walnut hulls (or other nut hulls)

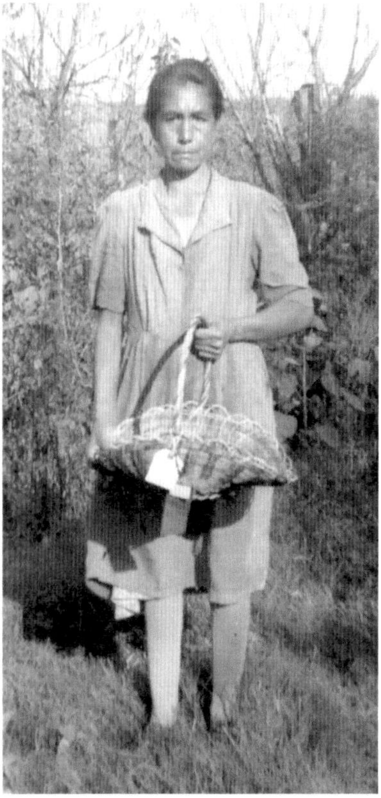

Lydia Adair won second prize for her flower basket at the Muskogee Fair in 1944. *National Archives at Fort Worth.*

give various browns to near black and bois d'arc wood chips or the dock plant provide a golden yellow.[73] A story in the *Joplin Globe* in 1966 noted that the Oak Hill Weavers used "dyes made at home from mulberry, walnut, pokeberry, and other plants of the region."[74]

Walnut hulls were crushed and boiled for optimal color. Following a soak in a dye bath, the weaving material should dry a minimum of twenty-four hours before use.[75] Color outcomes rely on various conditions such as season of gathering and type of soil feeding the plant. A mordant (often salt or baking soda) would be added to the dye bath to assist with color fastness, causing the color to bond with the material. Colors can be affected by the choice of the cooking pot. Metal pots, such as copper or iron, will leach trace amounts and interact with the materials in the pot, altering the color. Enamel coating, however, has no effect on the dye bath.[76] Generally, light, fluctuations in temperature and aging serve to disintegrate baskets. Most natural dyes are known as "fugitive," meaning they escape as time passes.

Millie Pigeon, reportedly ninety-five years old when interviewed in 1937, noted that her mother, Annie Christie, was born in Georgia and traveled the Trail of Tears. Pigeon's mother likely taught her to weave, and Pigeon continued the craft for perhaps three-quarters of a century.[77] Reading about early basket makers helps us realize there is a continuing thread in history rather than sterile lapses of time between events like Removal, the Civil War and statehood. People's lives typically span decades of historical changes.

Ollie (A-li) Duck, a Cherokee basket maker who came west on the Trail of Tears as a young woman, needed to purchase a horse in her elder years. According to a report by her grandson George Duck, she had no funds to purchase one, so she borrowed the money from a man known to lend money and was able to pay her loan by regularly presenting baskets to the lender, who marked off ten cents for each basket.[78] Basket-making skills might not have produced wealth, but baskets did provide the means to acquire necessary and useful items.

Eliza Sixkiller Padgett, born in 1870 and renowned locally in the first half of the twentieth century for her expertly crafted buckbrush baskets, learned basket weaving from her mother.[79] When Padgett's husband grew too old to work their farm, he helped her gather and process runners, and her baskets became their main source of income.[80] Padgett's baskets are found in the collections of the Philbrook Museum of Art,[81] the Five Civilized Tribes Museum[82] and the Oklahoma History Center.[83] A photograph of one of her baskets appears in the Smithsonian Institution's volume 14, *Handbook of North American Indians*.[84]

By perusing online census records, cemetery postings and a copy of a posted will, Padgett's mother is found to be Winnie Blackwood Sixkiller, born in 1844 in North Carolina, meaning she came west after the Trail of

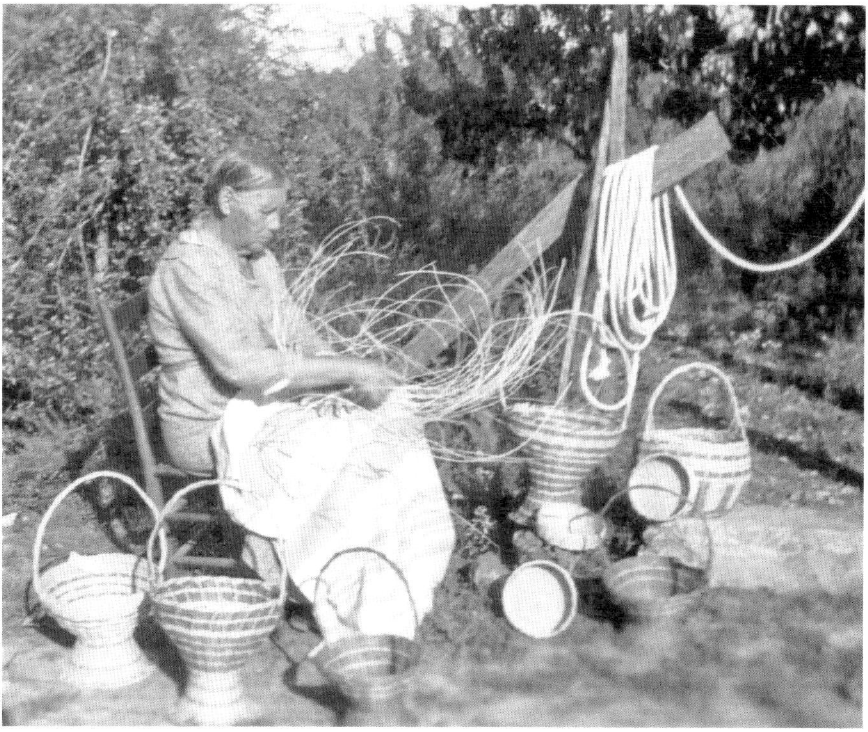

Eliza Sixkiller Padgett produced an array of buckbrush baskets in the first decades of the twentieth century. *National Archives at Fort Worth.*

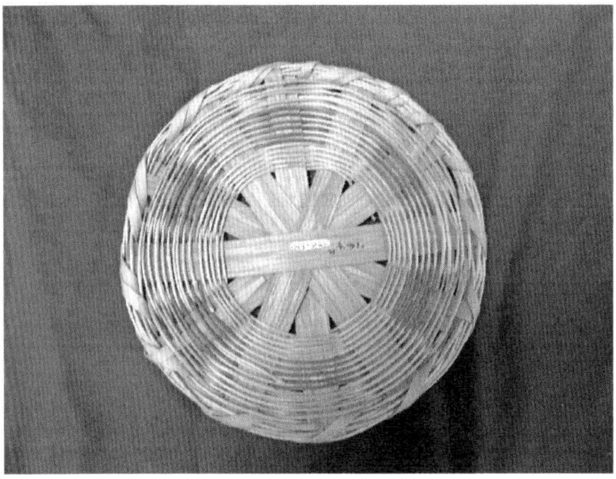

Left: Museum records note that Eliza Padgett used white ash as well as buckbrush in making this basket lid, dyed with walnut and bloodroot. *Five Civilized Tribes Museum.*

Below: Nannie Sixkiller Hogner, *center*, taught basket making to young Cherokee women as part of a federal jobs program. *Carl Albert Center Congressional Archives, University of Oklahoma.*

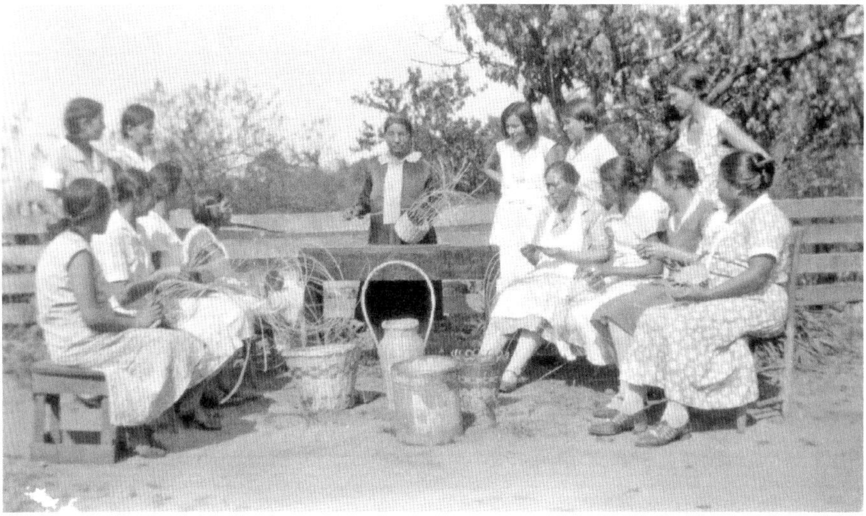

Tears exodus, which was not unusual. Eliza, the eldest daughter, was born in Wauhilla, Indian Territory. Her sister Nancy/Nannie Sixkiller Hogner, born in 1883, appears in a photograph showing her teaching a basket-making class. A basket made by Hogner is also in the Philbrook Collection.[85] In the old Eastern Cherokee homeland in past times, it had generally been assumed that every female would learn to make baskets; in the West, in newer times, that assumption began to erode, but not in the Sixkiller family and other families like theirs who persisted as basket makers, some continuing to the present time.

In July 1903, the following advertisement appeared in Muskogee's *Twin Territories* magazine: "When in Tahlequah Visit Hudson's Book Store." The ad text revealed the store carried Cherokee handmade baskets. Throughout

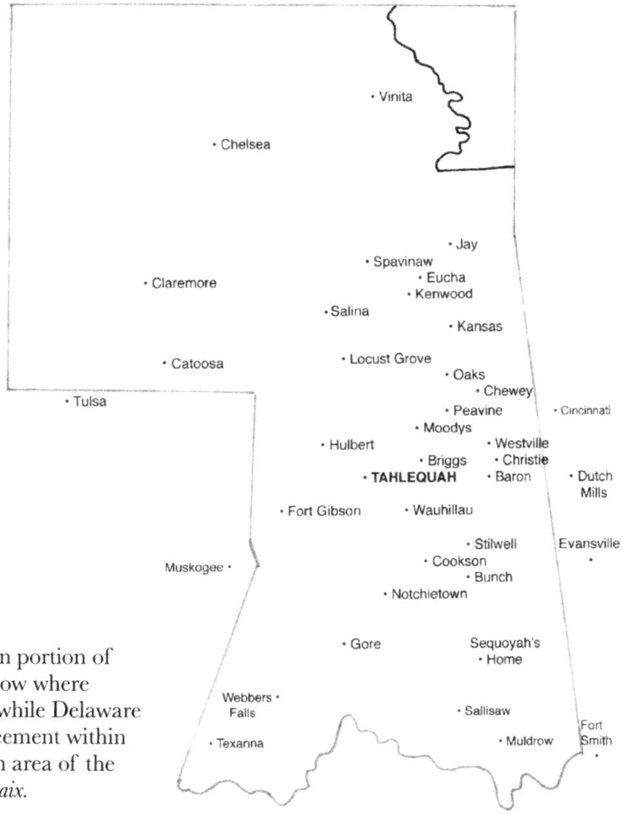

The extreme northeastern portion of the Cherokee Nation is now where eight other tribes reside, while Delaware tribal citizens live by agreement within the topmost northwestern area of the Cherokee Nation. *Jim Roaix.*

the following decades, various stores in Tahlequah, Stilwell, Jay and other communities within the Cherokee Nation sold Cherokee-made baskets, as some area stores still do today. Interviews with George Duck and Martin Blackwood reported that Cherokee baskets were often carried from Stilwell and Westville to nearby Arkansas towns such as Evansville, selling for ten to twenty-five cents apiece. Interviewee Jennie Hines reported that baskets were often sold for a nickel to a quarter, helping purchase groceries in Cincinnati, Arkansas.[86]

The invasive honeysuckle vine, *Lonicera japonica*, became established in East Coast states not long after being imported from Japan in the early nineteenth century. Eventually, the introduced honeysuckle found its way to Oklahoma, where Cherokee women began harvesting and processing its roots early in the twentieth century. Prepared honeysuckle runners resemble prepared

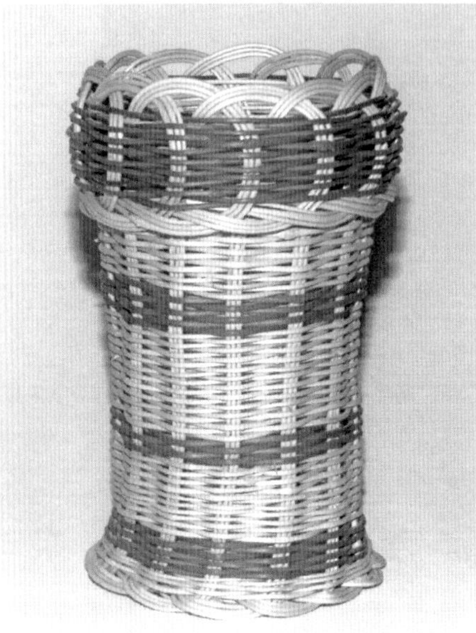

Lena Stick made this honeysuckle pen and pencil holder that can also serve as a vase. *Jim Roaix.*

buckbrush root runners but are generally more delicate in size. Mature runners two years or older are best harvested after the plants drop their leaves in the fall. Before weaving, the runners are boiled to remove the outer bark.[87] While indigenous honeysuckle exists (*Lonicera flava*), it did not become a popular basketry material, according to Matthew Anderson, the great-great-grandson of Eliza Padgett, because the invasive Japanese honeysuckle offers longer runners.[88]

It is not uncommon to see a runner basket employ sturdy buckbrush spokes secured with honeysuckle runners, especially at the basket bottom where space is tight. Some basket makers use local wood splints or rely on commercial flat reed (an imported processed Asian plant material) to serve as a framework around which the delicate honeysuckle runners are twined. Honeysuckle used alone is ideal for miniature and small, delicate baskets.

Both buckbrush and honeysuckle have knobby joints at intervals along the length of the long weavers, and both materials are currently popular with Oklahoma Cherokee basket makers. By looking for the knobby indicators on the material composing a basket, basket buyers can discern traditionally gathered materials from commercially processed weaving materials. Commercial reed is the machined inner pith of an Asian vine and generally winds up with occasional fine "hairs" of plant fibers splitting away from the core. The fact that it has no nodules and is exactly the same dimension from beginning to end makes the material appealing to some basket makers because it is easier to create an even and balanced basket rather than wrestle with varying widths of material interspersed with nodules, some of which bulge like knuckles.

ALLOTMENT, STATEHOOD AND THE DEVELOPMENT OF COLLECTING

1900–1920

With the passage of the Dawes Allotment Act, Cherokee citizens were allotted personal landholdings across the four-million-acre expanse of the Cherokee Nation.[89] In earlier times, Cherokee people performed their collective labors by working together in family groups. Traditionally minded Cherokee families had generally lived in extended family enclaves, anchored by a water source, where skills like basket making and wild plant harvesting were effortlessly taught through generational interactions. Federal officials, however, envisioned an expanse of active farms and ranches, dotted with growing commercial centers. In some cases, people were allotted land far from relatives.[90] As a result, many Cherokee girls began to grow up lacking daily interaction with basket-making grandmothers. Allotment paved the way for Oklahoma statehood in 1907, and the government of the Cherokee Nation was deemed closed at that time.

Lula Cochran Hair, born in 1904, was interviewed in 1969 in Hulbert and related that she had once had an old cane riddle basket that had been her grandmother's, but due to "moving around…I lost it so I haven't got it." She recalled how the basket had been used in removing the coating from corn kernels after soaking them in water with wood ashes.[91] Allotment diminished the effectiveness of the extended family and set many individuals adrift without necessary skills or an infrastructure to turn to.

The second Cherokee Female Seminary (the first accidentally burned down) was constructed by the Cherokee Nation in 1889 as a grand Romanesque-style three-story building and was transferred to the State of Oklahoma in 1909 to serve as the centerpiece of today's Northeastern State University in Tahlequah.[92] Afterward, the university transferred pertinent Cherokee cultural objects to the Cherokee National Historical Society, including a raffia basket made by seminary student Janana Ballard for display at the 1904 St. Louis World's Fair.[93] Raffia is an inexpensive palm product imported from tropical climates. The Cherokee Female Seminary had never been a vocational school (as were federally sponsored or missionary-led Indian schools). Instead, curriculum in the Cherokee Female Seminary had generally been intent on producing classically educated women. If basket making was taught, it was hobbyist non-Indian basket making like the raffia examples.

Ballard became a teacher at the seminary and is seen in a 1911 archival photograph published in the *Cherokee Nation and Tahlequah*[94] wearing a fashionable large hat that might have been made of buckbrush. Decades later, Sanford Cummings of Tahlequah was known to weave hats.[95]

Another seminary-connected basket was made by Susan Hider Soldier Glory, who became well established as a Cherokee basket maker in the early twentieth century. Although hailing from a traditional full-blood community, she attended the seminary system, as had her future husband, who attended at primary grade level. They probably both were recruited during a time when the Cherokee Nation's secondary schools were soliciting a more broadly representative student body, after having been accused of using common funds to cater to wealthy Cherokee families. Susan Soldier is not recorded as graduating from the school,[96] but she attained a successful level of accomplishment with her basketry skills, with two baskets preserved in the collections of the Philbrook Museum of Art[97] and one residing at the Cherokee Heritage Center.[98]

Allotment had not been cruel to all Cherokee citizens; many were able to stay where they already lived. The Chelsea-Alluwe Field, where the first Indian Territory oil well had been drilled in 1889, had created an island of wealthy Cherokee citizens who became bankers, ranchers and petroleum industrialists. Mary Erskine Clarke Hogue, a Chelsea resident and Cherokee citizen, bought her first Cherokee basket in 1913,[99] becoming perhaps the earliest aesthetically motivated collector of Oklahoma Cherokee baskets.

In 1914, a large, intricate Washo Indian basket, made in Nevada, sold for nearly $2,000.[100] The maker found a lucrative marketplace, selling her wares at a resort on Lake Tahoe in California. At that time, the highest price an Oklahoma Cherokee basket could warrant was less than $10. Over the years, Cherokee women in Oklahoma also began to make larger and more complicated works, and still they struggled to find buyers. Had they found a stronger market, they would have elaborated their skills into larger, more majestic creations.

Mary Hogue hoped to shine a bright light on Cherokee baskets in Oklahoma. Born in 1880, she married a successful cattleman and possessed financial resources and time to devote to visiting remote Cherokee basket makers. Hogue undertook the practice of visiting remote basket makers, buying a buggy load (and later a carload) of baskets and selling them at cost so she could return and purchase more, thus helping basket makers realize income they badly needed. Barbara Starr-Scott, former Cherokee council member, has fond memories of her father serving as a guide, taking Hogue into the hinterlands, accompanied by his young daughter Barbara, who went along on many of the shopping forays.[101] Mary Hogue supplied Cherokee baskets to a gift shop in Denver and provided Christmas-season shipments to a Sioux City, Iowa purchaser. She reported she had placed baskets in all forty-eight contiguous states, as well as in Ireland, Scotland and South America.[102] Additionally, she arranged for Neiman-Marcus of Dallas to carry Oklahoma Cherokee baskets.[103] She was not profiting but was dedicated to helping others gain fair money for their creations and furthering Cherokee culture and pride.

In April 1935, the *Tulsa World* published "Chelsea Woman Aids Cherokee Weavers in Marketing Wares," describing the large-scale efforts of Mary Hogue. A large photograph shows twenty baskets, big and small, all noted to be part of her personal collection. The article says, "An Indian woman may spend weeks patiently weaving baskets in her isolated cabin and find, when she is finished, that she has no way of disposing of her handiwork. She may trade it for a few beans in some tiny store, or to nearby white families for cast-off clothing, but the returns thus obtained are small compensation for the weary hours of manipulating roots and reeds into finished baskets."

Hogue's personal basket collection was composed of buckbrush baskets she bought primarily in the Eucha and Spavinaw communities.[104] Her daughter, Erskine Stanberry, inherited the collection along with the family home (the oldest Sears Home in the state) in Chelsea and explained how her mother developed an interest in baskets: "The first time we went over there, five families from Chelsea took all of us kids in covered wagons…the greatest thing that evolved was my Mother's learning about these Cherokee baskets…For a long time, they didn't know Mama by anything except 'the basket lady.'"[105]

Ted Foster, a local resident, filmed an interview in 2002 with the ninety-six-year-old Stanberry, capturing images of some of the collected baskets. When Stanberry died in 2005, Foster asked the managers of the estate about the baskets and was told only four baskets remained. Foster promptly purchased those baskets. He showed the film of the Stanberry interview along with his four purchased baskets at a meeting of the Pocahontas Indian Women's Club in Claremore on March 23, 2013.[106] The collection had also been photographed by historian and basket collector Marshall Gettys before Stanberry's death;[107] however, Gettys died early in 2015 before this author could view those photographs. Seven images of Hogue-collected baskets appear in a special basketry issue of *Cherokee Quarterly*.[108] Attempts were made to locate photographs of Mary Hogue, but none of the attempts was successful, although it is known that photographs of her once existed.

Sallie Rogers, sister of Oklahoma's great humorist, actor and statesman, Will Rogers, Cherokee, married Tom McSpadden and worked with several other Chelsea women, including Hogue, to support the craft of Cherokee basketry. McSpadden was noted as helping set up roadside stands on well-traveled roads.[109] Vinita, Chelsea, Claremore and Catoosa were located on the popular U.S. Route 66, operable in 1928. Sister-in-law Mrs. Herb McSpadden became the caretaker of the childhood home of Will Rogers and kept a supply of Cherokee baskets there to sell to tourists.[110] Will Rogers was known to purchase Cherokee baskets as gifts for friends and acquaintances.[111]

In addition to Hogue, another early Oklahoma basket collector was Clark Field, born in Dallas in 1882, who became interested in American Indian cultures in 1900 when he started working at an Oklahoma newspaper. In 1918, having founded a successful stationery business, Field began collecting and engaging in serious study of American Indian baskets, including Oklahoma-made works, and continued collecting for more than forty years.[112]

Field purchased some of his baskets from the Sequoyah Occupational Trade School near Tahlequah,[113] but most were obtained through interactions with the Oklahoma Indian Arts and Crafts Board office and primarily came from the Kenwood and Eucha areas.[114] Relocating with the Cherokee to Oklahoma were remnants of other southeastern tribes, the Euchie/Yuchi and the Natchez/Notchie, who had sought asylum among Creek and Cherokee villages in the East and still live among them today. Field purchased two Natchez baskets, a sifter and a tray, in 1937 from Wat Sam, who lived near Braggs, Oklahoma, in Cherokee territory.[115]

In 1938, oilman Waite Phillips donated his Tulsa villa to serve as an art museum, and Clark Field became a museum trustee, donating his basket collection of more than one thousand pieces in 1942 to the Philbrook Art Center, where they were exhibited.[116] Before Field's death in 1971, the Philbrook turned its focus to European art, and the majority of the Field Collection was loaned to the University of New Mexico, where it was eventually housed at the Maxwell Museum of Anthropology, financed by Field's daughter and her husband, Gilbert Maxwell, for whom that museum is named. The Field basket collection returned to Philbrook in 1986.[117] Thirty-four of the Field Collection baskets are Oklahoma Cherokee works,[118] and the museum has added several more Oklahoma Cherokee baskets since obtaining the collection.

Hogue and Field, along with other collectors, not only provided income to craftspeople, but when collectors were as discerning as Field and Hogue, they also helped keep the craft at the top of its game. Their collecting attracted other purchasers; their knowledge led to better records and information of the craft; their friendships with craftspeople and admiration for the beautiful objects validated the artists, inspiring the weavers to continue despite whatever challenges they may have faced.

In 1917, Oklahoma's first woman elected to the U.S. House of Representatives, Alice Robertson, along with her sisters, donated to the Oklahoma Historical Society the journals, letters and diaries of their grandparents, who had been pioneer missionaries among the Cherokee. At that time, Robertson also gave two Cherokee baskets to the society. The Oklahoma Historical Society also collected Cherokee baskets in 1920 and 1921 and took in three more in 1934. One of its baskets is currently displayed at Sequoyah's Cabin, and another is being shown at the Cherokee Strip Regional Heritage Center in Enid.[119]

While private collectors are important, museum collections can serve an even more important role by making their collections accessible to the public through exhibitions, publications, loans to other institutions and providing Internet access to their collections. It is essential for contemporary basket makers and members of the Cherokee community to see historical pieces, aiding cultural knowledge and mindfulness of the past from which we emerged.

POVERTY, DEPRESSION AND RECOVERY PROGRAMS

1920–1940

Polly Blackfox needed the services of a midwife sometime between 1924 and 1933. She created a beautiful, handled sewing basket with an interior small basket intricately interwoven into the bottom, all topped by a lid, and expertly formed of beautifully dyed buckbrush. The basket was presented to midwife Maud Peak of Beaty's Creek as payment for her services at the birth of a Blackfox child. The basket is now owned by Peak's great-grandson Ken Masters, and that basket led him to become a collector of Cherokee baskets at a young age, purchasing his first one, made by Jennie Sapp, when he was twelve years old. He remembers the Underwood arts and crafts store in Jay, run by Meda Underwood for forty years.[120] Again, we see how baskets served as currency and that there were various outlets for distributing baskets. However, local sales were generally slower than the weavers' capacity, and cash income was always hard to come by.

Sarah H. Hill's study, "Marketing Traditions: Cherokee Basketry and Tourist Economies," reports that annual incomes among Oklahoma Cherokee families averaged ninety-five dollars during the mid-'30s, inadequate for providing family necessities.[121] In 1934, Five Civilized Tribes Indian Services in Muskogee hired Orpha Young as a home extension agent to set up a basket-making program as a WPA effort to provide sources of income for area people. Young pointed out there was not so much a need to teach basketry as to encourage basket makers to adapt their products to new markets.[122]

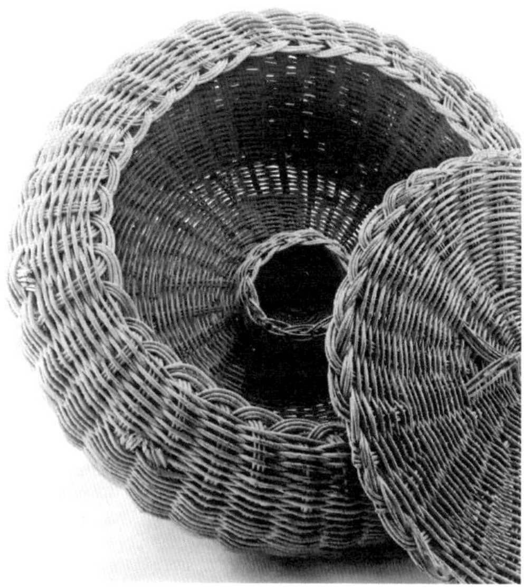

Polly Blackfox made and gave this sewing basket to Maud Peak for midwife services, circa 1930. *Ken Masters.*

In 1935, the Department of Interior was charged with managing the Indian Arts and Crafts Act (IACA), along with its oversight board (IACB). The purpose of the act was to encourage proliferation and protection of American Indian arts and crafts, with the goal of transitioning American Indians out of poverty. Hoping to fend off the lucrative international business of importing foreign-made "Indian" crafts for sale in souvenir shops, truth in advertising regulations were passed, and today enrolled American Indians use their individual Certificate of Degree of Indian Blood (CDIB) cards, issued by the Bureau of Indian Affairs (BIA), as proof of their status as recognized American Indians. The IACA was updated in 1990, and its BIA office continues to monitor the market.[123]

Alice Lee Marriott was hired to manage the Oklahoma IACB office, located in Oklahoma City. Born in 1910 in Illinois, having a BA in anthropology from the University of Oklahoma, she served as the field representative in Oklahoma from 1937 to 1942, when the program ended. Afterward, she would write more than twenty significant books about Oklahoma and American Indians and be named to the Oklahoma Hall of Fame. Her papers are preserved at the Oklahoma Historical Society.[124] Marriott's boss in Washington, D.C., was Rene d'Harnoncourt, who later became director of the Museum of Modern Art in New York City. On May 19, 1937, still new to her position, Marriott sent a long letter to the Washington office describing her recent visit to Gore, Oklahoma. She noted, "There is no arts and crafts tradition, so far as I can discover. The women do such plain sewing and patchwork as might be done by any farmwomen, and one makes buckbush [*sic*] baskets. I saw one of her baskets; nicer than any of those we saw in Muskogee, but was unable to get to her home."[125]

In a September 15 letter to the office, she wrote:

> *During the time that we were in Tulsa, Mrs. Mary Hogue, of Chelsea, Oklahoma, brought us, for examination, some very fine Cherokee baskets. These are made of buckbush* [sic] *runners, the same material that was used for the Cherokee baskets we examined in Muskogee, but are incomparably better than those in the Muskogee office. In fact, of their kind, I feel that they are better than the Choctaw baskets. I am looking forward to sending you a specimen.*
>
> *Mrs. Hogue asked me to visit her at Chelsea during the latter part of this month, and to make contacts with the women who are making these baskets. Only native dyes are employed, and I feel that it is extremely important to record these, as the colours are better than any other native dye colours I have seen in Oklahoma. The advantages of going with a person who is well-known to the Indians are obvious.*[126]

On the same date, Marriott wrote a second letter to d'Harnoncourt:

> *I made a trip up to visit Mrs. Hogue's sister, who has been working with her to collect and market the baskets. All they have gathered have, so far, been sold locally, or, through friends, to quite distant points. They both feel that the local market is exhausted. I do not: if it were, I should certainly have seen or heard of the baskets before now.*
>
> *At any rate, the quality of the work is absolutely amazing. When I expressed some surprise, I was told that if all I had seen were the specimens in Muskogee, there was nothing remarkable in it: those are culls. The women have been palming off on Mrs. Young the baskets Mrs. Hogue would not take, and those are the only ones we have seen.*[127]

The basket makers Marriott recorded include the following from the Eucha/Kenwood communities where Hogue actively assisted basket makers in selling their creations: Rabbit and Bessie Boney, Cullis and Lucy Buck, Aggie Mouse Budder, Allie/Ollie Budder and daughter Annie, Susan Soldier, Eliza Hair, Fannie Jumper, Anna Langley, Lucy Mouse, Annie Oosawee, Jenny Owens, Katie Proctor and Ella/Elsa Redbird. Cherokee men had joined women in making baskets.[128] Taylor L. Harry, born in 1867, was known to collect basketry materials for two of his sisters, one of them being Annie Oosawee.[129]

Marriott's marketing efforts included frequent visits to native communities across Oklahoma in search of the best crafted items, collecting and bringing

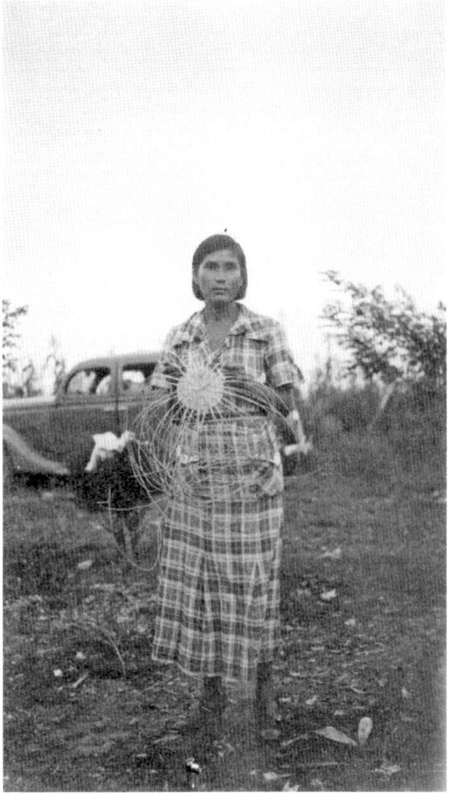

Lucy Buck holds the start of a buckbrush basket. *Carl Albert Center Congressional Archives, University of Oklahoma.*

Indian products to annual sales events, accommodating requests from groups wanting lessons and demonstrations, producing reports about Oklahoma native arts and facilitating payments to all involved.

"On Monday I got up to Eucha with Mrs. Young for a few hours, and saw Lucy Buck. I think that she and Kultus [*sic*], and little Clarke, will come to Tulsa and make baskets for the fair. This should be a big time for them; I do hope Lucy will enjoy it. They are to have their expenses and transportation paid, and the little family group should be quite an attraction," Marriott wrote to Mary Hogue in October 1937. Hogue had become her trusted advisor.[130] Cullis and Lucy Buck named their fourth baby Clark Hogue Buck, revealing how important the two collectors had been to the Buck family.

In 1938, a Tulsa Indian Exposition was held, and four hundred examples of Oklahoma Cherokee crafts, including an unknown number of baskets, were exhibited and offered for sale. The IACB hoped in 1939 to expand Oklahoma Cherokee basket markets to the West Coast during the San Francisco Exposition, but sales at that event proved to be slow.[131] Americans had been wooed by the romance of southwestern tribal arts as presented by exotically dressed Navajo, Apache and Pueblo tribes. Cherokee basket makers, on the other hand, no longer dressed in ethnic attire, and they were not receiving adequate notice in popular magazines. In the 1930s, rural Oklahoma Cherokee basket makers were visually ordinary in flour sack shirts and dresses and contemporary hairstyles and were unadorned by their traditional Cherokee copper or shell jewelry. Not living on a reservation, Cherokee people had less support and recognition.

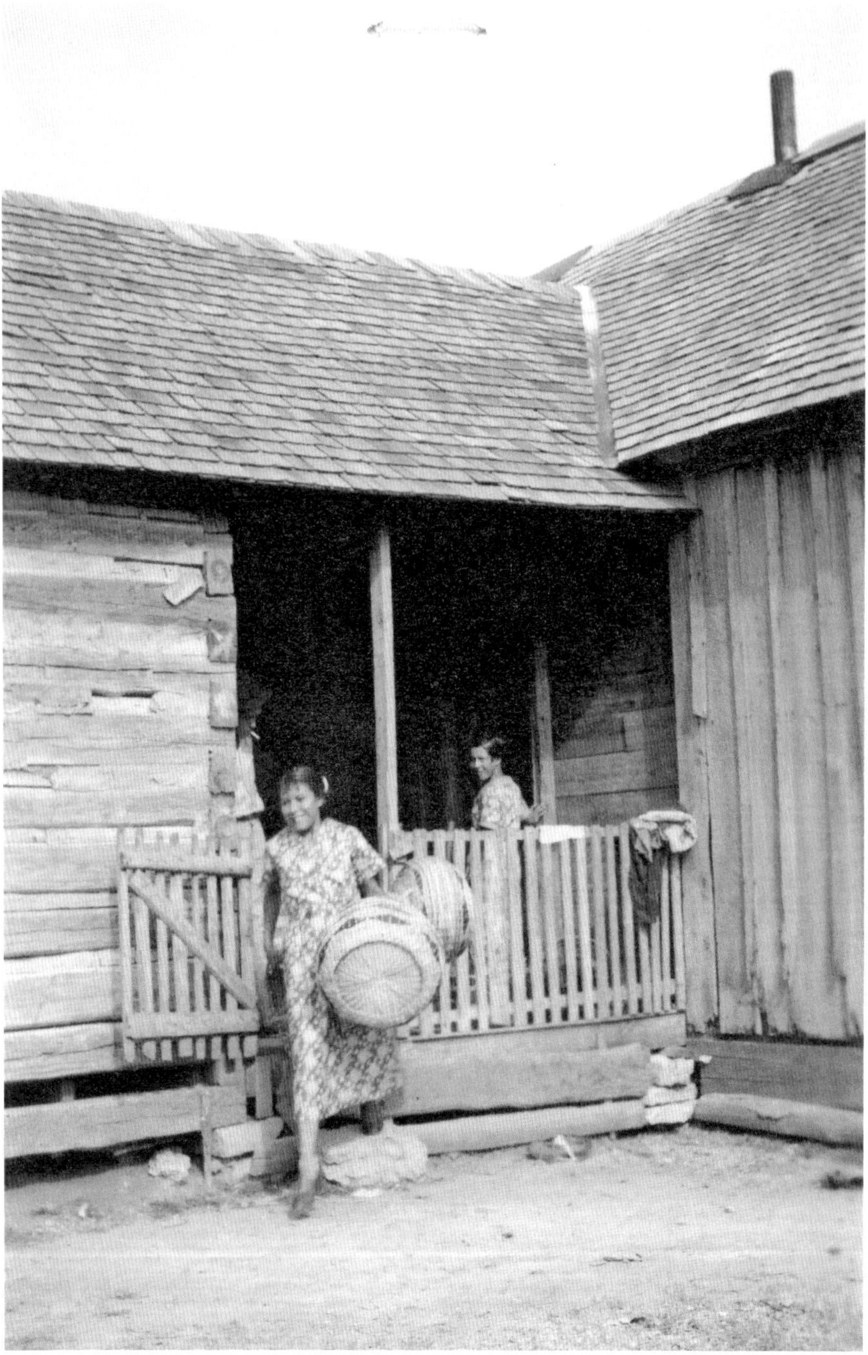

Rachel Tanner carries a batch of buckbrush baskets from her log home. *Carl Albert Center Congressional Archives, University of Oklahoma.*

Marriott's job ended in 1942[132] as war consumed the nation, and the IACB receded from its field offices to a centralized office in the nation's capital. Much later, three exhibition sites to promote Native American arts were built by the IACB: one each in Oklahoma, Montana and South Dakota. The facility in Anadarko, Oklahoma, has displayed the work of a number of Oklahoma Cherokee basket makers.[133] Marriott herself had collected Cherokee baskets and donated some to museums.

A September 8, 1940 Sunday feature of the *Tulsa World* titled "Indians Strive to Preserve Native Art of Basketry…Long, Hard Hours of Work Bring Only Slender Returns" focused on Mayes and Delaware County Cherokee women from Eucha, Kenwood, Jay, Salina, Spavinaw and Round Springs. Basket weavers cited were Rachel Bird, Rabbit Boney, Cullis and Lucy Buck, Annie Hair, Minnie Potter, Jennie Studie, Nancy Tanner, Rachel Tanner, Martha Vann and "the Proctors from Kenwood."[134]

For the reporter, the Proctors were too numerous to name individually. Katie Proctor and Eliza Proctor were Backwater sisters who married Proctors. Katie was the mother of Jennie Proctor Sapp, Celia Proctor Littledeer and Marie Proctor, all basket makers. There was Nancy Proctor, who married a Tanner and had three daughters take up basketry. Josie Proctor taught her six-year-old daughter Maggie to weave baskets.[135] Maggie Proctor was born in 1928 in Kenwood and later married an Alberty and moved to Tulsa, giving up basketry for a while, but then took it up again and became known for her work.[136] Basketry became one way to sustain tangible cultural connections when one was not able to remain in the community. When Maggie set up a sales table at Tulsa or other distant sites, she would also sell the crafts of her Cherokee relatives.[137]

The 1940 Tulsa article further reported, "Annie Hair, full-blood Cherokee woman living near Round Springs, makes 100 baskets a year, she says, and collects for them $40, sometimes. She would be glad to work even longer hours and make 200 baskets a year and so raise her annual income to $80."[138]

Of all the basket makers mentioned in this informative piece, only one was noted to work with cane. A photograph of Rachel Bird shows a lapful of split cane, and she is shown weaving a cane basket. When Millie Pigeon was interviewed in 1937, it was noted, "She has cane split on the porch, drying to make baskets."[139] The Philbrook Museum of Art has three cane baskets attributed to Nancy Wildcat of Gore, collected in 1941. While buckbrush may have become the predominant signature material used by Oklahoma Cherokee basket weavers, cane had obviously not been forgotten. It is not evident why Wildcat's basket rim and handle

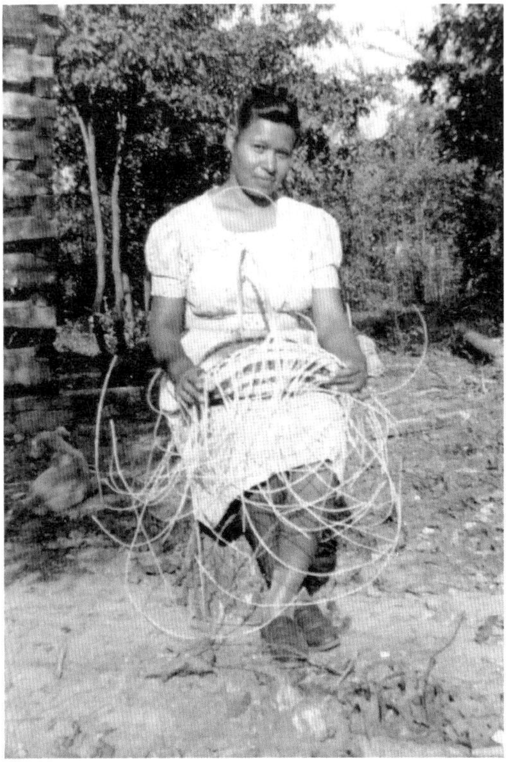

Left: Cecelia Proctor Littledeer, niece of Eliza Proctor, is shown in 1944 weaving a flower basket for weddings, funerals and events. *National Archives at Fort Worth.*

Below: Maggie Proctor Alberty, prolific weaver from Kenwood, moved to Tulsa as an adult and maintained family and Cherokee cultural connections. *Research Division of the Oklahoma Historical Society.*

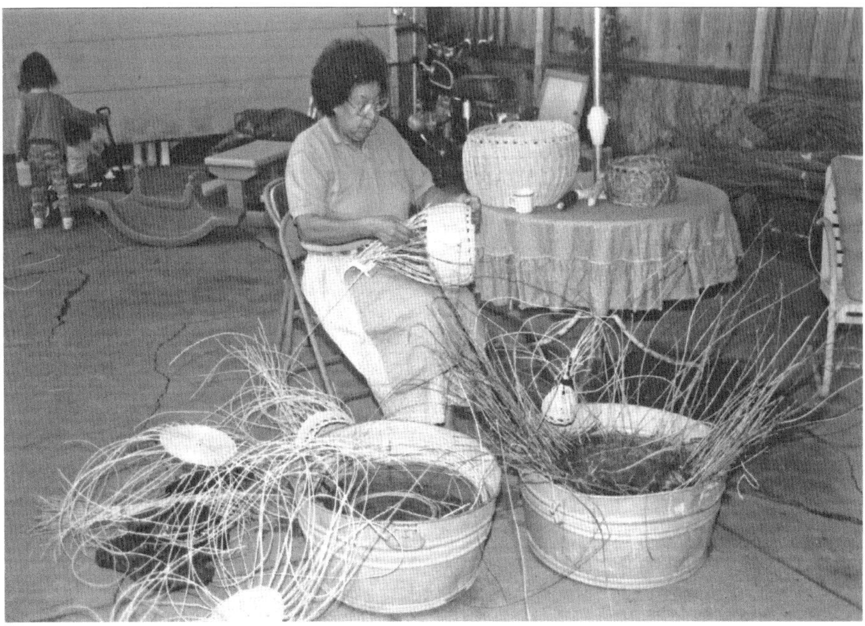

treatment more closely resemble Choctaw traits. Perhaps living at the southern end of the Cherokee Nation adjacent to Choctaw populations is reason enough.

The 1941 annual report of the WPA extension service mentions Fannie Jumper as an outstanding basket maker with the Brush Creek Community House. The report notes her as a teacher and demonstrator appearing at the Anadarko Fair, Muskogee State Fair and Oklahoma State University. Several of Jumper's baskets are displayed at the Delaware County Historical Society in Jay, Oklahoma.

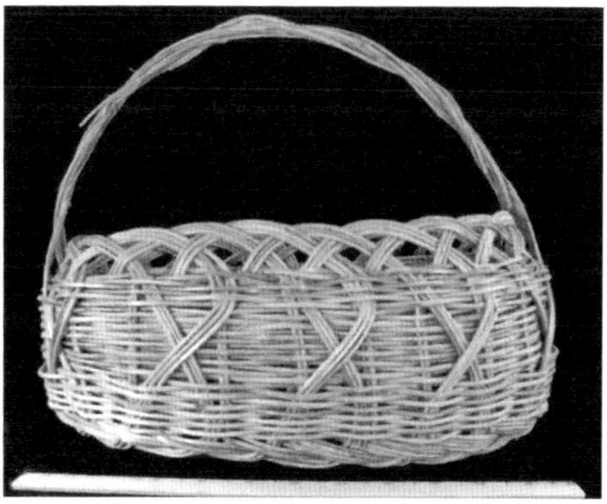

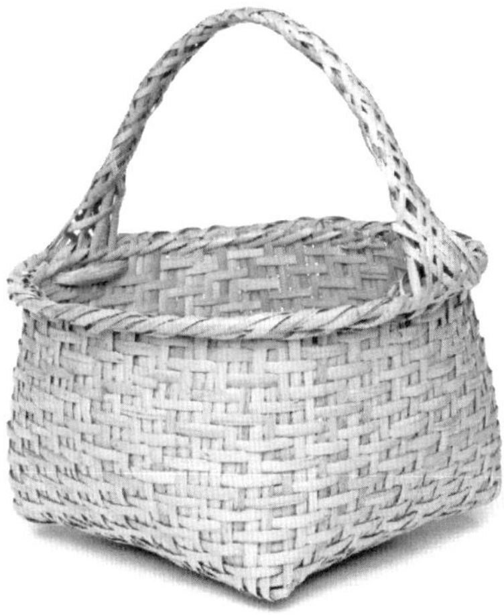

Top: This buckbrush basket made by Maggie Alberty is owned by a collector in Louisiana. *Louisiana Regional Folklife Program.*

Bottom: Nancy Wildcat of Gore made three cane baskets collected by Clark Field in 1941. *Philbrook Museum of Art.*

The 1944 annual report provides photographs of two Cherokee sisters, Annie Sawney Jones and Lydia Sawney Adair, with their prize-winning baskets and ribbons from the Oklahoma State Fair in Muskogee. The report cites the two sisters together sold more than fifty dollars worth of baskets over a nine-month period. The report also notes, "A market for the baskets has been one of the greatest problems for the weavers and that is where the Indian Office has been of aid to them."[140]

The United States Indian Services started a textile program in 1938 at Sequoyah Indian Vocational School, formerly a Cherokee orphanage, near Tahlequah. Before Removal, Cherokee women had achieved accolades for their loom-woven coverlets, and the textile program was designed to revive that art in hopes it would provide economic improvement to the continuously deprived Cherokee area. The first graduates of the textile program included

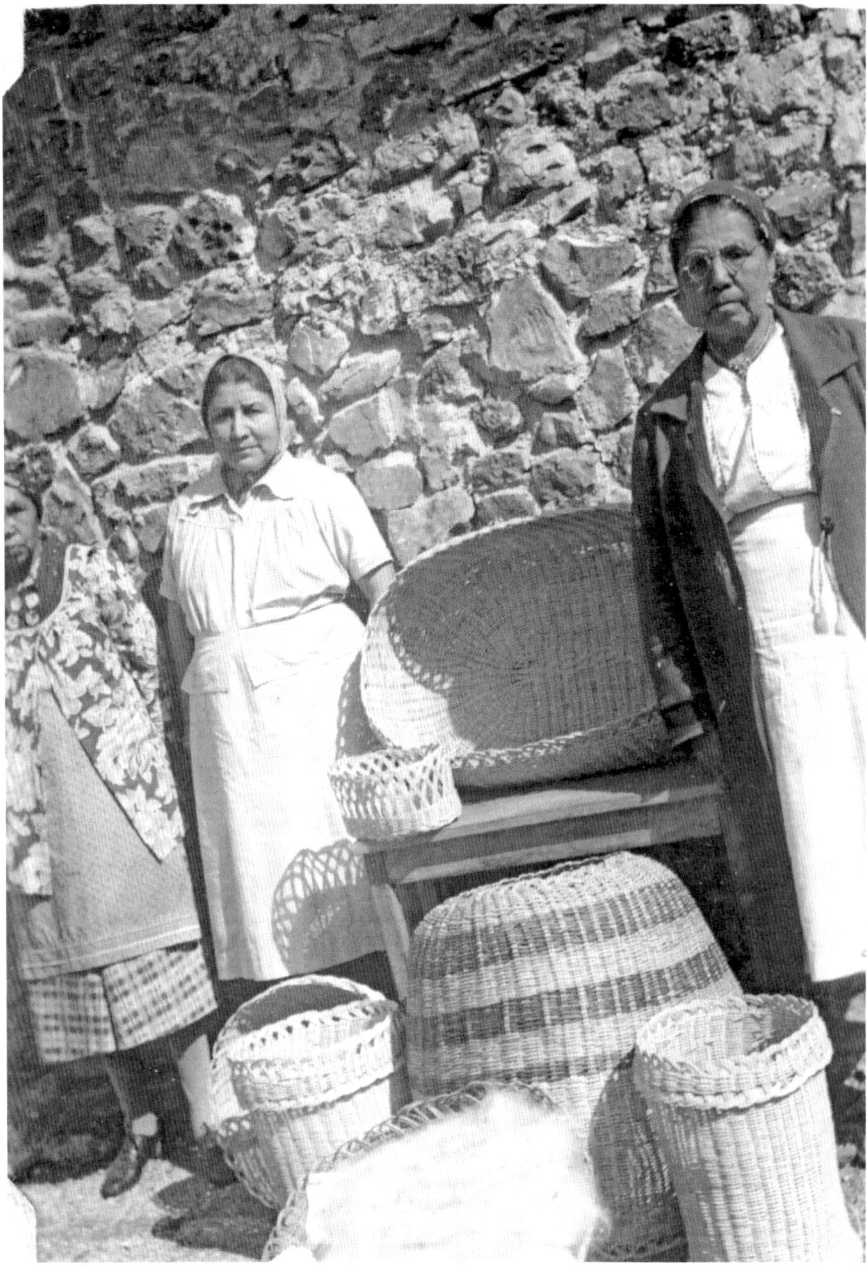

Fannie Jumper, *right*, was noted as the outstanding Cherokee basket maker in the 1941 WPA Extension Office report. *National Archives at Fort Worth.*

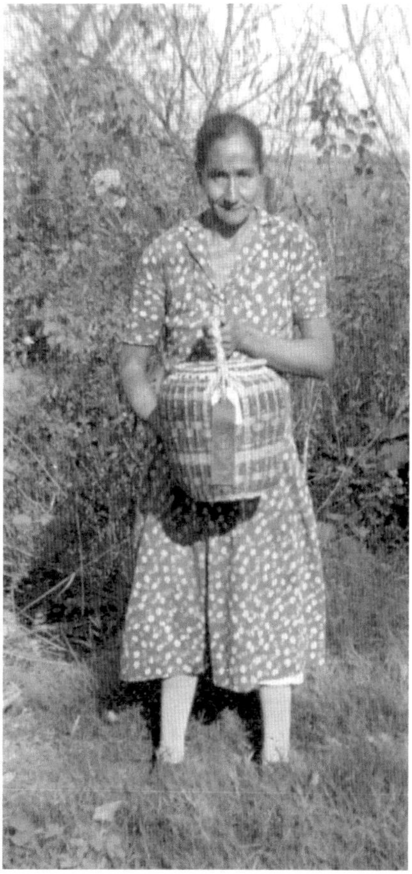

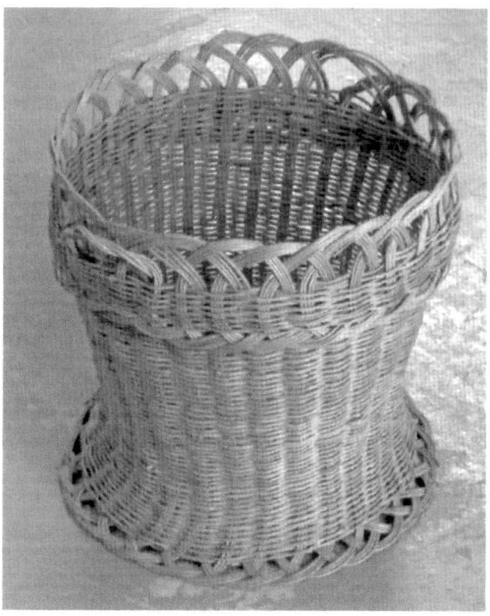

John Ketcher, who later became deputy chief of the Cherokee Nation of Oklahoma under Principal Chief Wilma Mankiller.

World War II intervened, and Cherokee men and women signed up for military duty. Contemporary basket weaver Regina Thompson described how some of the women who remained at home without their soldier husbands survived by producing baskets. "My grandmother [wove] baskets to put food on the table while my grandfather served in France during World War II," she reported. "My grandmother would create mid-size baskets for the market to trade for eggs, flour, chickens, and sometimes sewing material."[141]

John Ketcher returned to Tahlequah after serving in the navy during the war and began working for Bill Ames, who ran the Five Tribes Arts and Crafts program for the Bureau of Indian Affairs.[142] They spearheaded an effort to organize a cooperative called the Sequoyah Indian Weavers, which ultimately grew to a membership of 325 crafters, with perhaps half being basket weavers.

Top: Annie Jones won first prize at the Muskogee Fair in 1944. Her sister, Lydia Adair, won second prize. *National Archives at Fort Worth.*

Left: This Fannie Jumper buckbrush basket is exhibited at the county museum in Jay, Oklahoma. *Delaware County Historical Society.*

SELF-HELP STRUGGLES AND MUSEUM GROWTH

1940–1970

In 1941, J. Bartley Milam was appointed chief of the Western Cherokee by Franklin Roosevelt in order to pave the way for the Grand River Dam Authority to undertake dam building within former Cherokee boundaries. Milam took the opportunity to conduct efforts on behalf of Cherokee citizens and revived the Oklahoma Cherokee government.[143]

In 1948, Chief Milam asked author-historian Carolyn Thomas Foreman to produce a book, *Cherokee Weaving and Basketry*, and arranged to pay for the publication of the thirty-three-page booklet by Star Printery in Muskogee.[144] Thus, the first book about Oklahoma Cherokee baskets found its way into print, and a copy may be viewed in the special collections of Northeastern State University or at the Muskogee Public Library. Foreman became a collector of baskets, donating many to area museums as they developed in the state. Several baskets remain as decorative items in Foreman's home, now a house museum in Muskogee known as the Thomas-Foreman Home.

In 1958, Oklahoma historian Muriel Wright wrote "American Indian Corn Dishes," published in the *Chronicles of Oklahoma*, in which she reported, "The set of three baskets—the fanner, riddle and containers—for sifting and cleaning the ground corn are still seen in some Indian homes in remote parts of Eastern Oklahoma." She noted that Cherokee fanners were often made of white oak wythes (Old English for flexible woody pieces).[145] We learn from her observations that traditional baskets continued to be made and used into the middle of the twentieth century.

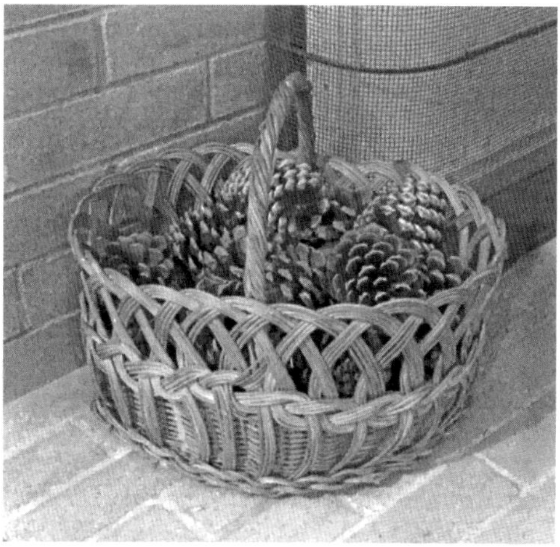

Right: Cherokee baskets are displayed in the historic Grant-Foreman Home in Muskogee. In 1948, Carolyn Grant Foreman wrote the first book on Oklahoma Cherokee baskets. *Jim Roaix.*

Below: A portion of an old map depicts Oklahoma, with Kenwood designated as a reservation. *Jim Roaix.*

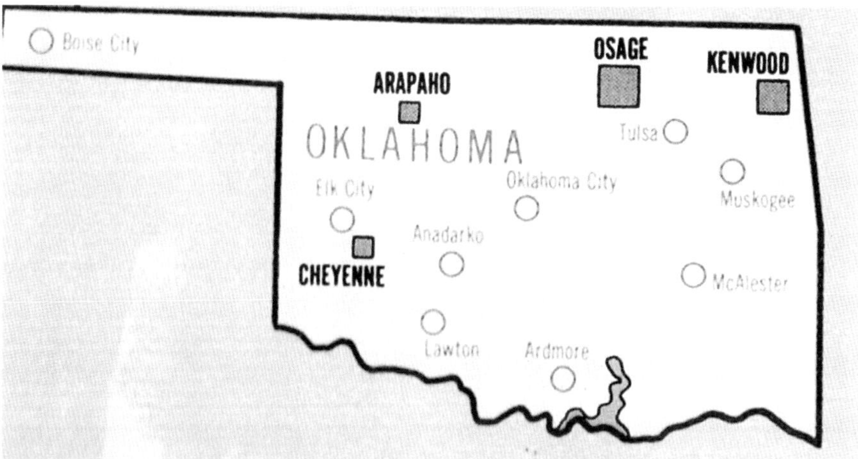

Kenwood, a small traditional Cherokee community, had come to be known as the center of Oklahoma Cherokee basketry, partially aided by the efforts of Alice Marriott, Mary Hogue and Clark Field, who promoted the crafts of the area. An undated paperback picture booklet, *Indians of the Southwest*, includes a centerfold map of fourteen western states. The Oklahoma portion of the map notes four "reservation" markers: Cheyenne, Arapaho, Osage and Kenwood. While the word "reservation" has a distinct governmental definition, people often view things independently, and during the time the Cherokee Nation was dormant, many considered Kenwood to be a reservation.[146] "Kenwood Reservation" was used in the following account of a 1959 Miami, Oklahoma newspaper story: "Fairview School in the Kenwood Reservation southwest of Jay has 15 children enrolled, 12 of who are Cherokee. They are so poor, according to reports, they have never had a real Christmas." The report goes on to tell about Oklahoma's Miami Beauty College students taking a holiday meal to Kenwood students, along with gifts. The article describes a boy who had played with a stuffed football-shaped burlap bag being happy to receive a real football.[147]

Kenwood probably felt like a reservation to those who lived there, and apparently it also seemed so to those outside the area. Kenwood was, to its credit, making a mark in basket making. In 1962, Clark Field donated a basket made by Kenwood's Lucy Mouse to the Smithsonian's National Museum of Natural History. It is an unfinished double-wall buckbrush basket made to demonstrate how the double weave is accomplished.[148]

Meanwhile, the Sequoyah School's textile program had produced competent Cherokee loom weavers eager to market their coverlets. In 1946, a simple frame building was moved from Camp Gruber to Briggs, three miles east of Tahlequah, to serve as a sales outlet and work center for the newly organized Sequoyah Indian Weavers.[149] While the organizing group had been composed of loom weavers, all Cherokee crafters were invited to sell their wares at the building, and basket makers brought in their inventories.

One of the Sequoyah Indian Weavers ledgers is preserved in the Cherokee Heritage Center archives and reveals that basket makers received from $0.85 to $4.50 per basket in 1943, depending on size, quality and style.[150] At first, basket makers' names were not noted in the ledger; however, names did appear on price tags, and some baskets can be found in collections or in antique shops with tags still attached. Carolyn Foreman studied Sequoyah

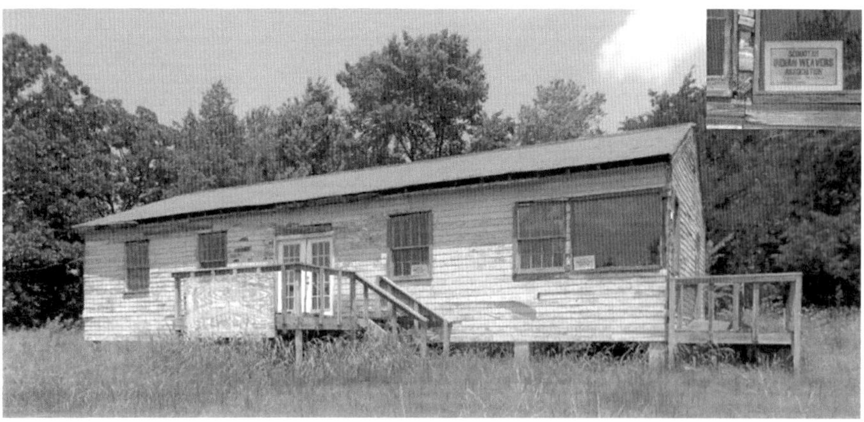

The Sequoyah Weavers obtained a Camp Gruber building in 1946, using it for craft sales and workspace at Braggs, east of Tahlequah. *Jim Roaix.*

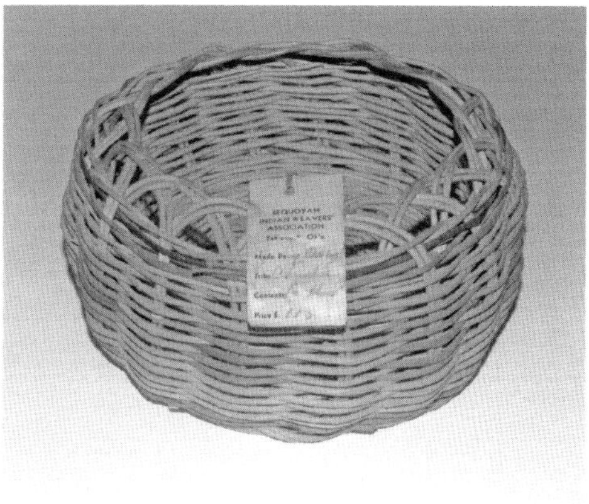

A Sequoyah Weavers sales tag reports Jenny Owens made this buckbrush basket. *Jim Roaix.*

Indian Weavers sales records and found there were 163 basket maker members in 1948 who sold a total of 1,370 baskets that year, an average of 8 baskets each.[151] In 1951, basket makers Mary Bark and Sally Lacy provided small baskets sold at $0.75 apiece while a lunch basket would command $3.00 ($3.00 at that time equates to $27.00 in today's economy).[152]

The idea of working together to sell Cherokee crafts expanded to neighboring communities. By 1951, there were a total of three Sequoyah Indian Weavers locations: Briggs, Bull Hollow and Oak Hill. Ultimately, the number of community groups producing crafts grew despite most not having a community building. Many crafters enjoyed meeting and working in hosting homes at Jay, Rocky Ford, Stilwell, Peavine, Strawberry Springs and elsewhere.[153] In 1954, federal support for the loom-weaving training program stopped. In 1962, the Briggs building shut its doors. The next year, its members placed crafts on consignment at Western Hills Lodge on Grand Lake and in Hind's Department Store in Tahlequah.[154] The building survives with its sign in the window, and over the decades, there was talk about reviving the enterprise, but the location is not on a main artery of traffic.

The Oak Hill Weavers continued to operate for a longer duration. In 1965, the IACB noted the purchase of two small baskets from Oak Hill Weavers, paying $1.50 for a small plain buckbrush basket, maker unknown, and $1.25 for a partially dyed small basket made by Lucy Weeley, both now in collections of the Smithsonian's National Museum of the American Indian.[155] In today's cash value, the price of Weeley's basket equates to $9.26.[156]

In 1969, thirty Cherokee families were involved in establishing the Bull Hollow Cherokee Arts and Crafts Association,[157] and in 1971 it was reported that the Sailboat Bridge Association agreed to fund the shop to promote tourism in the area.[158]

The Five Civilized Tribes Museum was organized in 1955 in the old Indian Union Agency building, built in 1875 in Muskogee, a county seat

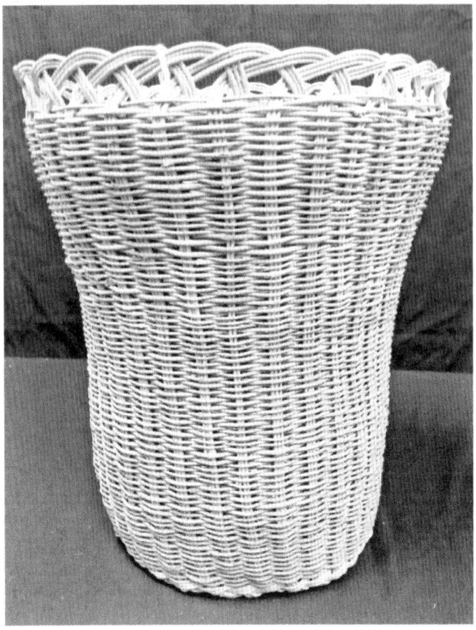

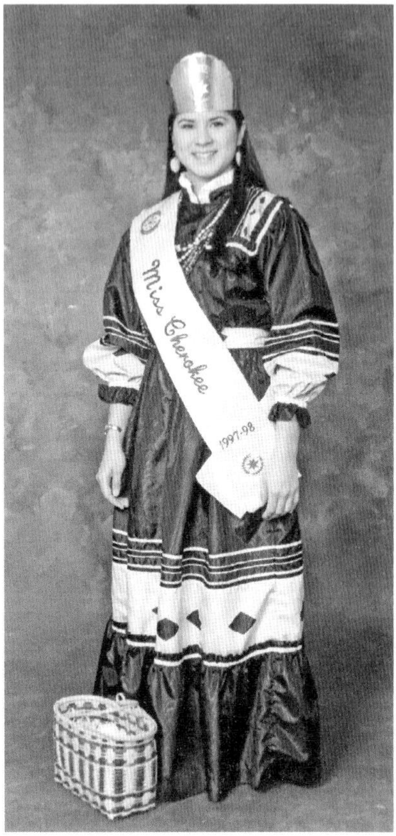

Above: Lucy Mouse produced this fourteen-inch-tall double-woven buckbrush wastebasket now in the collections of the Five Civilized Tribes Museum. *Five Civilized Tribes Museum.*

Right: Christy Sequichie, winning the Miss Cherokee title in 1997, was presented a Cherokee purse basket. *Cherokee National Historical Society.*

in Creek Indian territory, adjacent to the border of the Cherokee Nation. The museum began collecting materials, developed exhibitions, opened a salesroom and undertook a successful annual art show in 1967. Today, several Cherokee basket makers regularly participate in the museum's continuing art competitions and annual market, Art Under the Oaks, and also provide inventory for the museum's gift shop.[159]

The first Cherokee National Holiday was held in 1953 to celebrate the anniversary of the 1839 reunification constitution joining Old Settlers with Trail of Tears arrivers.[160] In 1957, the Tahlequah Chamber of Commerce began coordinating a Miss Cherokee Holiday contest. In 1959, an unidentified publication ran a photograph of the competitors that year, all holding Cherokee basket purses.[161] The basket purse has long been made by Eastern Band of Cherokee crafters and is typically made of oak splints. It swings from a pair of carved oak handles with carved oak hinges locked into the weaving of the basket. Traditional dyes of walnut or butternut and bloodroot (or commercial dyes representing those colors) are used in traditional weaving patterns. The basket purse is handy for holding items accumulated during formal public appearances, such as printed programs, contact cards and mementos.

In 1962, honoree duties expanded for the young women winning the competition, and the title became simply Miss Cherokee. Cherokee leaders purposely avoid the word "princess," which became anathema long ago to Cherokee sensibilities due to incessant references by non-Cherokees claiming to have a grandmother who had been "a Cherokee princess." Over time, the Cherokee Nation became wholly responsible for the pageant. Sporadically through the decades, purse baskets made in North Carolina were presented to Miss Cherokee, but in very recent time, pageant producers have arranged to have baskets for winners of three age categories made locally, and preference is given to National Living Treasures. The practice of the presentation basket becoming part of the pageant is another boon to Cherokee basket makers and firmly places basketry in a role of prominence in Cherokee culture, since each year's basket appears in the pageantry of parades, stage events and photo opportunities.

The *Stillwell Democrat-Journal* newspaper archive can be accessed online and provides a spotlight on basket making in the area near the Arkansas border. On August 29, 1960, Virginia Martin sold baskets at the Fort Gibson Arts and Crafts Show, appearing in a photograph with Congressman Ed Edmondson, who was noted to be admiring her work. The article also reported that she sold several baskets at the event. From an obituary of a relative, we learn that Martin was a sibling of George Fourkiller, who was named as a Cherokee National Living Treasure for basketry in 1992.

In 1964, the *Stilwell Democrat* included several basket-related announcements. On April 9, it reported, "In the quiet of Cherry Tree community, an old art is being revived." The story noted that Stella Livers had taught a basketry class, including history of Cherokee baskets, based on studies published by ethnographer Frank G. Speck. Mention was made of Cherokee use of diagonal and chain patterns and double-wall production. On September 10, it was reported that Lula Gibbons was gathering buckbrush, and on September 17, the newspaper stated, "If you happen to see someone in the vicinity of Baron walking down the road with a load of switches you will know it is someone interested in basket making. The switches are probably buckbrush runners."

On October 1, 1964, the Stilwell newspaper reported that Lula Gibbons spent four days at the fair at Muskogee and one day took along Babe

Blackwood, who "just recently learned to make baskets and was fortunate in finding a sale for one of her baskets."

Stilwell's Mulberry Craft Center took advantage of annual dogwood tours to sell baskets, pottery and weavings.[162] In 1968, federal Indian education reports noted that thirty-two trainees at the center received a total of $500 for their work, and participating craftspeople earned collectively $2,546 from sales of their products.[163] In addition to several women weaving baskets, it was noted, "among the men are Charley Swimmer, Wilson McLemore, and George Fourkiller, all of whom also spent part of their time weaving baskets at Mulberry."[164]

In 1973, the Stilwell newspaper noted that the Indian Program of the Oklahoma State Extension office had sponsored a four-day workshop at Lula Gibbons's home in Baron, with more than a dozen women attending. Participants gathered and prepared buckbrush runners and produced a completed basket. The class was referred to as an annual event, and the report also noted that Cherokee baskets would be available at the Stilwell Strawberry Festival.[165]

While most opportunities for Oklahoma Cherokee basket makers seemed destined to come and go, fifty years ago one came and stayed. Just as the Cherokee Nation government was being resuscitated after having been dissolved at statehood, the Cherokee National Historical Society (CNHS), a private nonprofit organization, was established by a group of Cherokee and non-Cherokee citizens in 1963. Their first concern was to preserve the ruins of the original mid-nineteenth-century Cherokee Female Seminary. After stabilizing a sample of surviving brick columns of the former multi-story Greek-style building, the society developed a living history village and hired people fluent in Cherokee language to demonstrate basket making and other crafts.[166] Due to the construction of five large energy-producing and Tulsa water-source dams from 1924 through 1953, scenic and recreational lakes and state park facilities began to create tourism in the area. The CNHS developed a

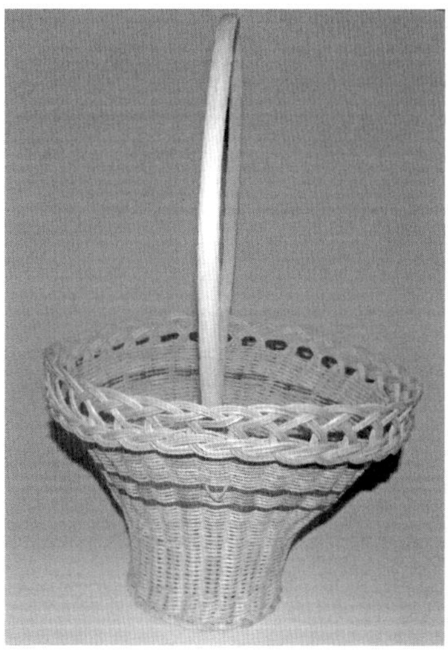

This commercial reed flower basket was made in the new millennium by Anna Sixkiller Huckaby, Cherokee National Treasure. *Jim Roaix.*

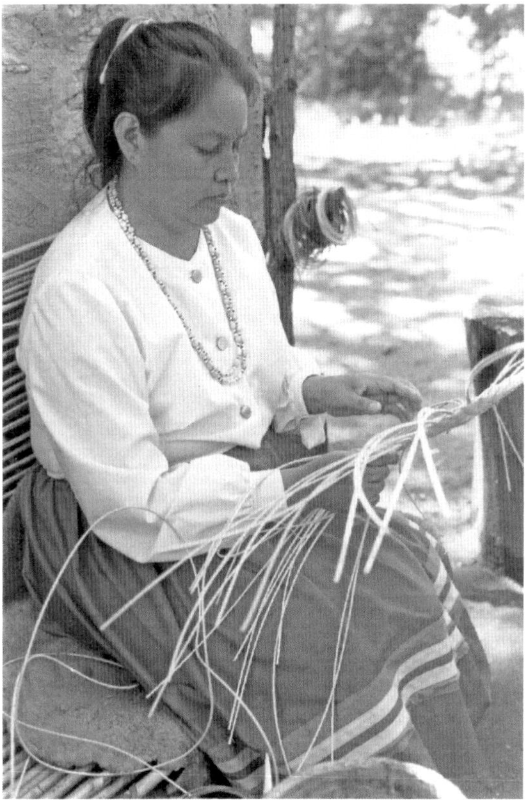

In 1963, the Cherokee National Historical Society created an Ancient Village, and Anna Sixkiller later demonstrated basket making there. *Cherokee National Historical Society.*

professional-quality museum with gift shop and informative galleries, tapping into tourism, and continues to function as an educational institution half a century later.

Today, the visitor complex is known as the Cherokee Heritage Center (CHC). Cherokee National Living Treasures associated with working in the demonstration village have included Ella Mae Blackbear, Anna Sixkiller, Thelma Forrest, Lena Blackbird, Nadine Wilbourn, Bessie Russell, Kathy Van Buskirk and Rachel Dew.[167] The demonstration village program made it possible for several basket makers to actually make a living based on their craft. The opportunity still exists in the replacement version of the living history village, now called *Diligwa* (Tellico/Tahlequah).

ART SHOWS AND EXHIBITIONS DEVELOP

1970–1985

The Cherokee Heritage Center (CHC) hosted its first Trail of Tears Art Show in 1971. Originally, only fine art pieces depicting Removal scenes were accepted into the show, but when the center developed a second annual art show—the Homecoming Art Show—beginning in 1996, both shows accepted baskets along with other traditional arts. The CHC also provides a variety of workshops, with one or two each year focusing on basketry, taught by experienced Cherokee basket makers.

In 1980, the Philbrook Art Center in Tulsa announced a new exhibition titled "Native American Art at Philbrook." Regrettably, a large portion of the Clark Field Collection was on loan to the Maxwell Museum of Anthropology at the University of New Mexico and would not return to Tulsa until 1986.[168] Five Cherokee baskets are referenced in the exhibition catalogue, but nothing informs the reader as to whether the baskets originated in North Carolina or Oklahoma. Only one photograph of a Cherokee basket is shown among the five numbered baskets, and it appears to be North Carolina made. The only basket maker name cited is known to be from North Carolina, and no buckbrush baskets are cited. The catalogue cover is a large photograph of the Washo Indian basket Field collected after extending his collecting beyond Oklahoma tribes.[169] Unfortunately, baskets made by Oklahoma Cherokee crafters were not being touted at a time when recognition of Cherokee baskets could have greatly provided a boost to the ever-neglected and struggling Oklahoma Cherokee basket makers.

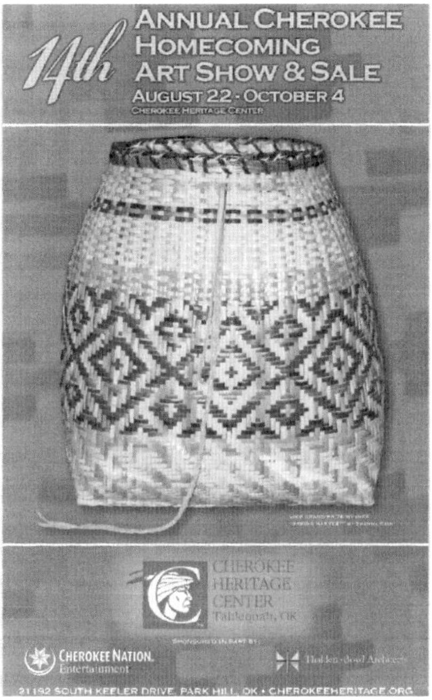

The Cherokee Heritage Center announced its 2009 art show with a photo of the previous Best in Show, a cane basket by Shawna Cain. *Cherokee National Historical Society.*

Around the time of the Philbrook exhibition, Principal Chief Ross Swimmer obtained a grant to send Thelma Forrest and Mildred Justice Ketcher to visit the Eastern Band Cherokee in North Carolina to study basketry efforts there. They came back with information about crafts cooperative management, along with a collection of patterns of traditional designs used in cane basketry by the North Carolina Cherokee.[170]

Richard Sattler, author of *Basketry of Southeastern Indians*, lamented in 1984, "In Oklahoma, where no stable market for baskets developed… there are few well-known weavers."[171] While the situation for Oklahoma Cherokee basket makers had begun to improve, due to decades of hard work by various individuals, Oklahoma Cherokee basketry still had not caught the kind of traction the baskets of the Southwest, Northwest, Northeast or North Carolina enjoyed.

In 1986, William and Sarah Turnbaugh published their acclaimed book *Indian Baskets* and included images of nineteen North Carolina Cherokee baskets but showed no images of Oklahoma Cherokee baskets. Their book, however, did not ignore Oklahoma Cherokee baskets. Instead, it disparaged them. The Turnbaughs noted what they considered to be a lack of continuing traditions among all the relocated Oklahoma tribes, and while they mentioned that both Qualla Boundary and Oklahoma Cherokee basket makers were using honeysuckle, they made no mention of buckbrush use.[172]

"Oklahoma Cherokee wicker baskets have decorative, structurally manipulated rims and additionally are so brightly colored due to white influence that they do not look 'Indian' to some collectors," wrote the Turnbaughs.[173] Were the authors saying white buyers preferred bright colors and that Oklahoma Cherokee basket makers gave up their own tasteful color values to cater to white buyers? It is a sentence that doesn't

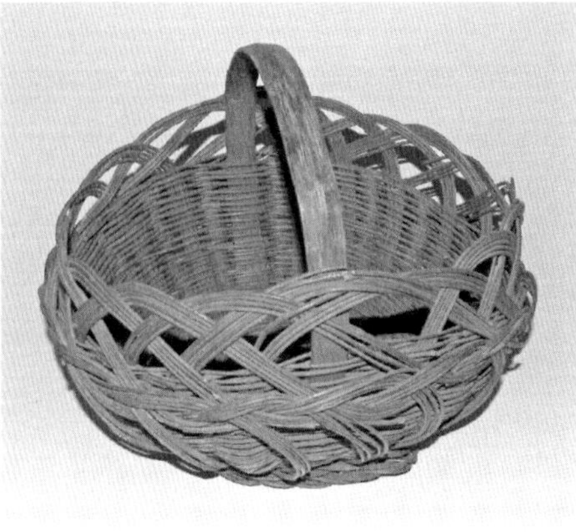

Old Oklahoma Cherokee baskets can be found in antique shops in as well as adjacent to the Cherokee Nation. *Jim Roaix.*

seem flattering to either party in whatever way one discerns its meaning. Initially, "decorative, structurally manipulated rims" sounds complimentary, but when attached to a phrase decrying not looking Indian enough, it seems to intend a negative judgment.

Further, ignoring the long continuous history of Oklahoma Cherokee basket making, the authors wrote, "Most of the basketry made by the relocated Oklahoma peoples dates only to the Contemporary Period."[174] That statement is not true, and if they thought it was true, why not at least include a contemporary example in their lavish book?

During this time, antique stores grew in number as town center businesses diminished. For many, antiquing became a hobby. As baskets aged, as households modernized, as inheriting generations had no idea of what they had inherited, old Cherokee baskets showed up in resale shops, most often in towns bordering or on the periphery of the Cherokee Nation. Many of them would be sold at prices higher than they had originally garnered. Most often they had darkened with age and become brittle. Most often the maker's name had not been noted. But sometimes a buyer can be lucky and find a basket with an identification tag still with it, and occasionally he may find a basket that has been stored for safekeeping and still has visible dye colors.

Meanwhile, for Oklahoma Cherokee basket makers, the increasingly difficult effort to sustain something invisible and misunderstood by the outside world continued to take its toll, and the disappointment experienced by Oklahoma Cherokee basket makers grew into an ever larger barrier between them and their goals.

RECOGNITION OF OKLAHOMA CHEROKEE BASKETS

1985–1990s

The very same year the dismissive Turnbaugh book was published, Oklahoma Cherokee basketry finally gained recognition. Ella Mae Blackbear burst onto the scene to alter the trend of national publications ignoring Oklahoma Cherokee baskets when one of her works was selected to tour the nation from 1986 through 1988. Ralph T. Coe, noted museum curator of American Indian art, traveled to Tahlequah in 1982 searching for indigenous pieces to include in a major national traveling exhibition, "Lost and Found Traditions: Native American Art, 1965–1985." Coe happily purchased one of Blackbear's double-weave baskets at Tah-Mels Indian Jewelry store in Tahlequah. The impressive buckbrush basket's photograph is captioned in the exhibition catalogue with a descriptive entry praising Blackbear's work.

Coe wrote, "Many Western Cherokee baskets are small tourist items, but this double-woven example…by one of the finest contemporary weavers is a tour de force of buckrush [*sic*] weaving."[175] Buckbrush or buckbush are common names for the plant.

Blackbear, born in 1930 in Salina, Oklahoma, had learned to make double-woven runner baskets by watching her mother, Elsie Wickliffe Backwater, born in 1892.[176] Blackbear became known for producing large, sturdy buckbrush cradles. In 1982, videographer Scott Swearingen met Blackbear at a Gilcrease Rendezvous Art Show and arranged to produce the video *Cherokee Basketmaker* detailing her life and work.[177] Although there were Cherokee Nation departmental photographs taken of Blackbear, they

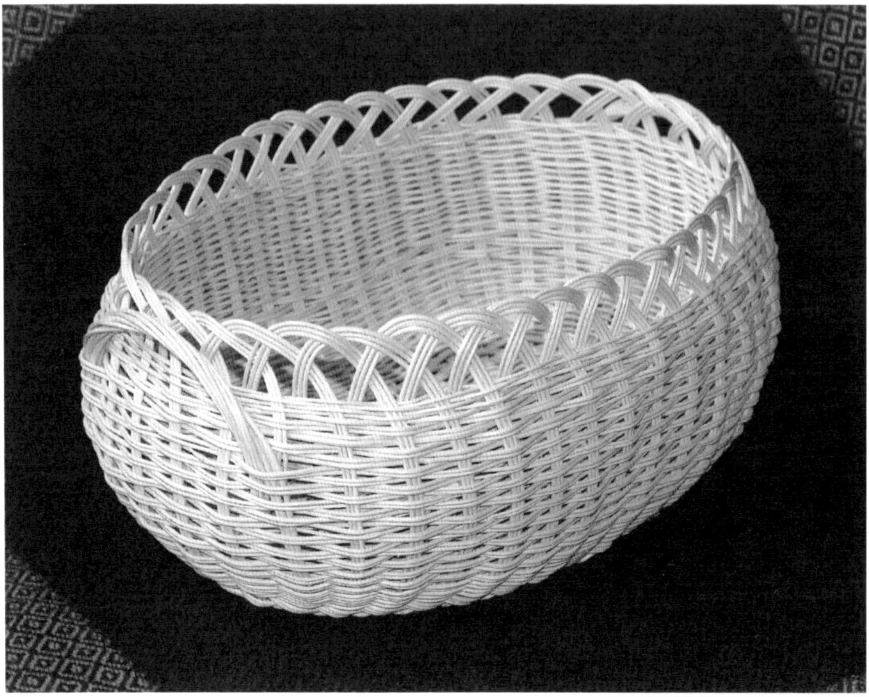

Ella Mae Blackbear wove tight, strong buckbrush baskets like this one in a private collection. *Jeff Davis.*

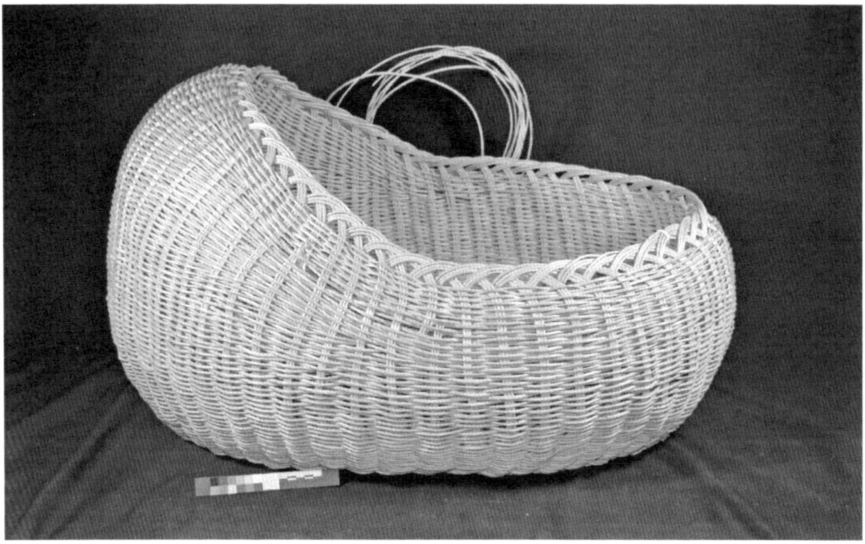

Ella Mae Blackbear became the first Oklahoma Cherokee basket maker to gain national attention. She became known for large buckbrush cradles. *Cherokee National Historical Society.*

were not located by this researcher. In 1990, Blackbear was among the first basket makers to be honored as a Cherokee National Living Treasure. Fellow honored basket makers that same year were Mary Foreman, Sally Lacy, Stella Livers, Jennie Sapp and Maxine Stick.[178]

The Cherokee National Treasures program was initiated in 1988 out of a federally funded Lost Arts Project undertaken by the Cherokee Nation.[179] The program continues to recognize and honor Oklahoma Cherokee people who achieve and perform traditional skills and share their knowledge. The United Keetoowah Band of Cherokee Indians, also headquartered in Tahlequah, developed a similar award called Tradition Keepers. In addition to previously mentioned honorees who had worked in the CHC living history village and the original six inductees noted in the above paragraph, other members of the distinguished honorees include, alphabetically, Shawna Morton Cain, Rosie Chewie, Vivian Garner Cottrell, George Fourkiller, Betty Christie Frogg, Betty Scraper Garner, Cindy Hair, Kathryn Kelley, Mildred Justice Ketcher, Linda Mouse-Hansen, Eunice O'Field and Marie A. Proctor.[180]

In 1988, Charlie Soap, husband of then-chief Wilma Mankiller, was managing a Cherokee program called the Gadugi Project, and Carolyn

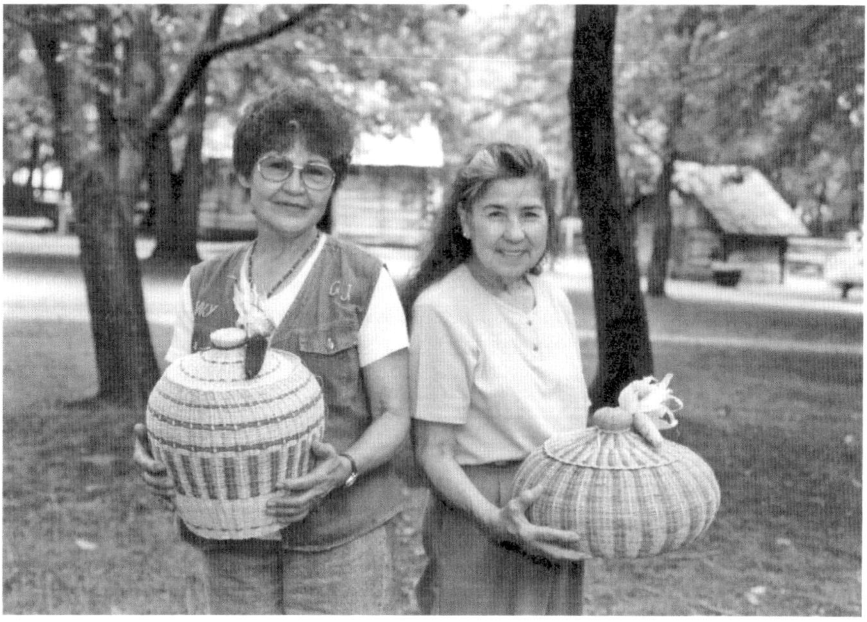

Bessie Russell, *left*, and Lena Blackbird, Cherokee National Living Treasures, were honored for their basketry skills. *Cherokee National Historical Society.*

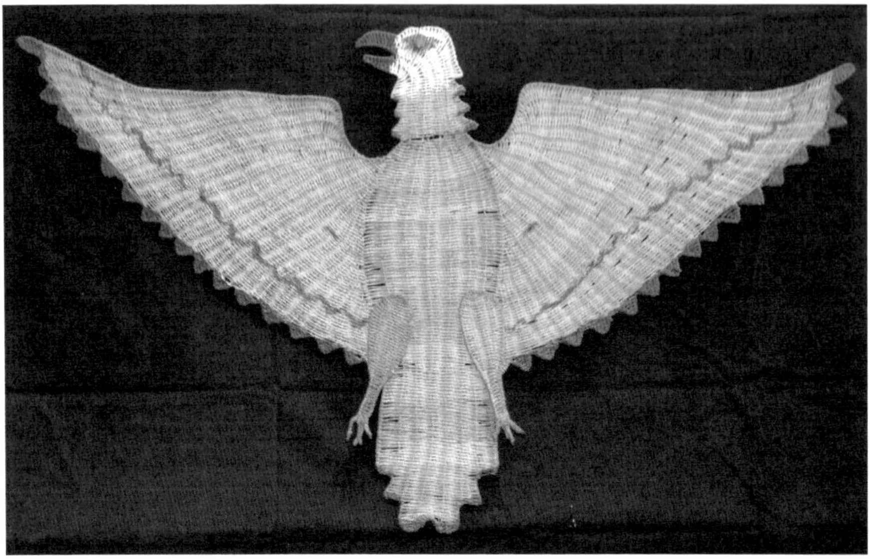

Made by basket weaver Jennie Sapp, this Eagle wall hanging displays creative ingenuity. *Lisa Rutherford.*

Chumwalooky became the manager of an initiative called the Kenwood Arts and Crafts Cooperative. Basket makers Ella Mae Blackbear and Maxine Stick became active participants.[181] Stick, born in 1931 in the Eucha/Jay area, learned basket making from her mother, Aggie Mouse Budder, born in 1902. Stick became known as a maker of large buckbrush clothes hampers and market baskets. The National Museum of the American Indian holds four of her baskets in its collections.[182]

The Kenwood Cooperative announced in 1990 that it had forty members and the cooperative's reputation had spread from Santa Fe to Phoenix to the Smithsonian. Representatives of the group were reported to have traveled to North Carolina and New Mexico, attending a total of twenty-five shows during the year. The Wheelwright Museum in Santa Fe produced an exhibit about the basket-making Kenwood community.[183]

Carolyn Chumwalooky described the beginning of the Kenwood Cooperative: "I knew about a few people here who were good artists, but when we started asking people to bring in their artwork and crafts, I couldn't believe some of the things that came out of these hills."[184] She now operates her own Cherokee arts shop in Salina, west of Kenwood. Her greatest focus while working with the cooperative was marketing, and she advised artists to maintain high standards for their products and to price works realistically based on time expended and quality. She reserved sales tables for the group at festivals and organized the staffing of events.[185] Although the program proved helpful to basket makers, the cooperative effort was not able to sustain itself without further funding. The help the program provided, however, continues to aid individuals with contacts they made during the program and with the business savvy they gained.

A recent tour of Kenwood, provided to the author by Ken Foster, who devoted the 1970s to Cherokee Nation arts programs, led to informative conversations with Kenwood residents as they talked about continuing sales links in Dallas and about Las Vegas buyers who visit familiar Kenwood basket makers once a year to purchase large numbers of baskets for resale. For many, Kenwood is still the place to go for fine and numerous baskets.

An important role played by Cherokee herbalist Arlene (Arlie/Ollie) Levi Sack, born in 1913, was gathering raw basketry materials during her herb-searching treks. Sack would then sell the materials to basket makers who couldn't roam the countryside. A few such men and women were known to gather and sell harvested basket materials. They also played an important role in the sustainability of basket making.[186]

Non-Indian experts had long ignored or misunderstood Oklahoma Cherokee basket making, but indigenous researchers began to emerge in the 1980s, propelled by a desire to make up for past omissions and transgressions made by publications regarding American Indian crafts. American Indian researchers were more likely to interact with native communities, and they understood how tenuous and important the survival of native arts has been for impoverished tribal communities.

Claude Medford Jr., a Choctaw man, had forged a career as a cane basket maker and often traded his baskets to collect the crafts of other indigenous people. He arranged for his collection to go to an anthropology museum in Natchitoches, Louisiana, and after his death, his treasures were placed there on exhibit. A 1990 catalogue of his extensive collection, *The Old Ways Live*, includes a photograph of a Jennie Sapp buckbrush double-woven basket while noting two Joyce Johnson baskets and one Eunice O'Field hominy-washing basket.[187]

Lakota artist Nadema Agard-Smith's grant-funded *Southeastern Native Arts Directory* included biographical statements and photographs of Oklahoma Cherokee basket makers Mavis Doering, Mary Foreman, Dora Grayson and Thelma Forrest, along with examples of their work.[188]

CONTEMPORARY CHEROKEE BASKETRY ISSUES

As basket competition venues grew, issues about quality and traditions arose. For some judges, the use of commercial reed (an Asian machined product) and boxed dyes devalued handcrafted traditional arts and misrepresented indigenous skills and heritage. Elder basket makers, on the other hand, cited the difficulty of gathering and processing materials. Some efforts were undertaken to assist elders, but the problem was never adequately solved. The issue of materials and quality was not a new issue, and the debate continues.

Mary Stone McClendon, known as Ataloa, affiliated with Bacone College in Muskogee, wrote in 1937 that it was "difficult however to convince the basket makers that vegetable dyes are to be preferred over analine."[189] Richard Sattler wrote in 1984 regarding Oklahoma Cherokee baskets in *Basketry of Southeastern Indians*: "Quality and production are improving although several weavers work extensively with commercially purchased materials."[190] The use of natural local materials versus commercial imported materials became a contentious issue.

Commercial round reed and its counterpart, commercial flat reed, were becoming the materials of choice for many Oklahoma Cherokee basket weavers due to limited access to gathering areas. Additionally, gathering and processing is especially difficult for the primary basket makers, elderly women. Commercial reed is the preferred material for use in basket-making classes to avoid wasting precious gathered material on neophytes. Soon there was a generation of upcoming Cherokee basket makers who had never harvested or worked with indigenous materials. The living history village at the Cherokee Heritage Center relied on commercial reed for daily demonstrations in order to avoid over-harvesting natural materials. One might think basket makers working at the village would be interested in obtaining their own good materials to work on competition baskets, but interruptions from visiting groups do not generally lead to prize-winning creations.

Commercial reed is the inner core (pith) of the rattan palm vine (*calamus* species) and is harvested and processed in Asian lands. The outer skin is sliced off in quarters to serve as rattan weavers for furniture, leaving the skinless pith available for shaving into round or flat reed. Lengths can be purchased at twelve feet or more, and round reed can be obtained in widths ranging from 1/8 inch to 5/8 inch.[191] Run through machines, the width of commercial reed remains consistent from end to end, unlike domestic wild plant runners, and that consistency makes the weaving easier to manage. Stripped of its natural coating, however, it will never acquire a polished patina like that of local Oklahoma hand-gathered materials, but it does readily take a dye. Commercial reed tends to be "hairy" as fibers separate from its pared surfaces.

Another commercial product is processed cane. One form is called chair cane, made for use in weaving colonial-style chair seats, and another commercial form is called Hamburg cane, which lacks the outer cane coating.[192] These imported materials are processed in large-scale production and prove less appealing for savvy collectors who discern the imported material, as do the most astute art show judges who generally favor hand processing of traditional indigenous materials. Indigenous cane, however, is getting scarcer due to increased agriculture, cattle grazing, lakes inundating canebrake habitat and housing expansion. Further, the gathering and preparation of natural materials is an arduous undertaking, especially for elders.

Vivian Garner Cottrell, having learned basket making from her mother, Betty Scraper Garner, noted that she and her mother stopped using commercial materials in the 1970s when they turned to gathering honeysuckle and buckbrush and making and using natural dyes. Living in Tahlequah, they arranged their baskets in the family den and sold from their home, relying on various shopkeepers and hotel clerks to send inquiring buyers to them.[193] Recently, Cottrell has started gathering river cane along the Illinois River near her home in Chewey.[194]

Cottrell related an amusing tale from her childhood about selling her baskets to a vendor who paid for them by their weight. When her mother

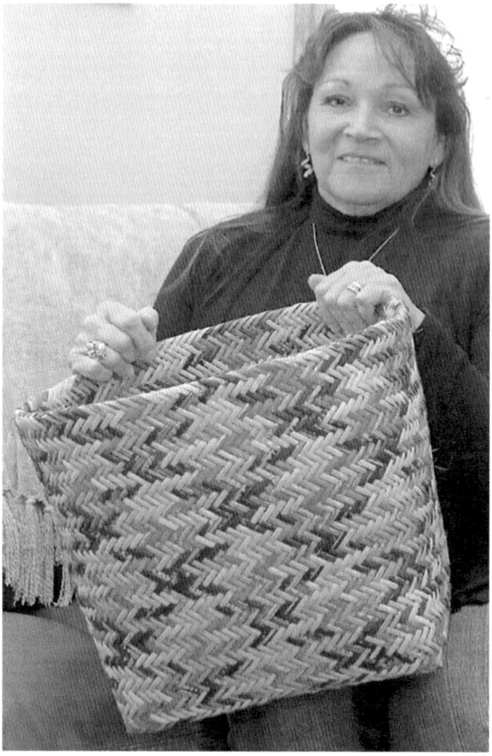

Right: Vivian Cottrell holds one of her cane baskets. *Will Chavez,* Cherokee Phoenix.

Below: Vivian Cottrell, a Cherokee National Living Treasure, weaves a complex cane basket. *Ronald C. Cottrell.*

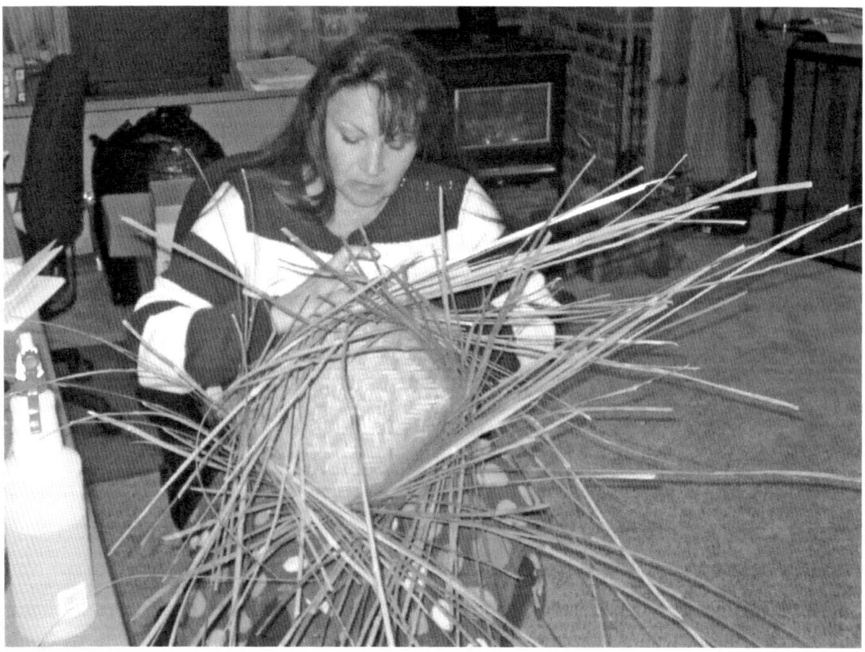

heard how little she had been paid, she told her daughter to soak them in water before she visited that vendor again. She did and received her fair pay.[195] At times it is hard for basket makers to set their own prices, but when the market is brisk, one can raise prices and test what buyers will pay. Mother and daughter both were honored with the title of Cherokee National Living Treasure.

In 1990, Mavis Doering's Cherokee baskets were commanding handsome prices, ranging from $250 to $1,400. Located in Oklahoma City in the center of Oklahoma, she could access art shows and galleries and became a hit at the nearby Red Earth show and sale. She had experienced Cherokee community life in childhood and understood the dichotomy of her success compared to the frustration of so many Cherokee basket makers hidden in country lanes and lacking the resources to take their wares to distant shows.

She noted, "I know a lot of excellent basketweavers in the Cherokee nation, but they're not visible and they've not gotten the prices for baskets they should have. One of the goals I've always had is to perhaps by being more visible and getting more for my baskets to help increase what they get."[196]

THE NEW MILLENNIUM AND CASINO CASH

2000–PRESENT

God bless the child that's got his own."[197] The Cherokee had "their own" several times during their journey as a socio-cultural political group of people, but their financial independence was repeatedly stripped away and subverted to benefit others. Events such as Removal, the Civil War and land issues such as forced sale of Cherokee Outlet, the forced Allotment Act and a series of lake and military installations seizing land all served to keep Cherokee citizens unsettled and adversely manipulated. Currently, outsiders view the Cherokee in Oklahoma as a wealthy tribe, but no one can foresee how long the current golden goose—casinos—will profit Cherokee communities. Cherokee government efforts have made good strides in developing alternative means of support, as well as strengthening the self-sufficiency of its widespread population through training, education, housing, infrastructure, health services and jobs. While individual poverty exists, increased opportunities and higher education attainment have jumped forward.

The Cherokee Nation has had a newspaper of its own, off and on, since 1828, and currently the *Cherokee Phoenix* is published monthly, distributed worldwide and offers online news. The *Phoenix* regularly reports art show results and publishes studies of various Cherokee basket makers. Additionally, homegrown Oklahoma Cherokee artist America Meredith, now living in Santa Fe, is publisher/editor of the new *First American Art Magazine*, and Lisa Snell, Cherokee, is editor of *Native Oklahoma*, a monthly publication that also carries arts news. Cherokee connections with publications help keep information flowing in and out of the Cherokee Nation, benefiting Cherokee basket makers.

In 2001, the Philbrook Museum of Art announced an exhibition entirely devoted to the Clark Field Collection, titling the show and its book "Woven Worlds." The impressive exhibition ran for two months in Tulsa and then traveled to other museums, including the Eiteljorg Museum of American Indians and Western Art in Indianapolis. This time not only were Cherokee baskets on exhibit, but the Tulsa museum also organized a Woven Worlds Basket Weaver's Market Place, with Oklahoma Cherokee basket weavers in attendance. The museum took the opportunity to add six Oklahoma baskets to its collection from four of the guest basket makers: Mary Aitson, Peggy Sanders Brennan, Kathryn Kelley and Mary Stone. The exhibition catalogue includes eight regional studies, with Marshall Gettys authoring the Oklahoma piece, which includes two photographs showing a total of five Oklahoma Cherokee baskets, with one identified as made by Sally Lacy.[198] The book includes a full listing of all the baskets from Clark Field's collection, and on pages 225 and 226, Oklahoma Cherokee baskets are listed with notations of use, material, maker, date collected and where collected when known.[199]

As the new millennium got underway, the Cherokee Nation, composed of more than 300,000 citizens, began offering free learning opportunities for its citizens regarding Cherokee history, language and culture. The emphasis on culture continued when the Cherokee Nation Holiday Art Show started in 2005, offering the show's highest cash prizes for winners in traditional arts categories. That same year, the Cherokee Nation launched a nationwide American Indian art show and sale, Cherokee Art Market, now held annually at the Cherokee Hard Rock Casino complex at Catoosa, near Tulsa. That show attracts American Indian artists from across the nation by paying handsome awards and encourages Oklahoma Cherokee artists to compete nationally without incurring the expenses involved in long-distance travel.

In 2007, Susan C. Power published *Art of the Cherokee: Prehistory to the Present*. The book's contemporary Oklahoma basketry section focuses mostly on Oklahoma Cherokee basket makers not residing within Cherokee jurisdiction boundaries.[200] Many Cherokee citizens living in the Oklahoma Cherokee heartland believe the issue of how representative one might be as a Cherokee is based on family links, cultural experience, knowledge and intimacy with the Cherokee-populated place one hails from. It is thought that those who continue residence in Cherokee communities might best represent Cherokee culture by virtue of their continuing involvement in ever-evolving Cherokee life through daily interactions with Cherokee people. Consequently, when authors rely on Cherokee informants who are not residing in Cherokee communities, the resulting information is not seen locally as representative of the core community. Additionally, as local people prosper from attention, it enriches Cherokee communities with feelings of shared pride and has more influence on financial improvement for the local economy. Such are the issues of modern-day American Indian life.

Most Cherokee artists initially were not able to mount websites, and cellphone service has been erratic in Oklahoma Cherokee areas, so it is understandable that researchers have had difficulty contacting Cherokee craftspeople. However, future researchers focused on Cherokee arts should now be able to find the best representatives for the research they are currently conducting. If Oklahoma Cherokee artists in the homeland were exceedingly hard to find a decade ago, today that is no longer the case due to the opening of the Cherokee Arts Center (CAC) in 2011.

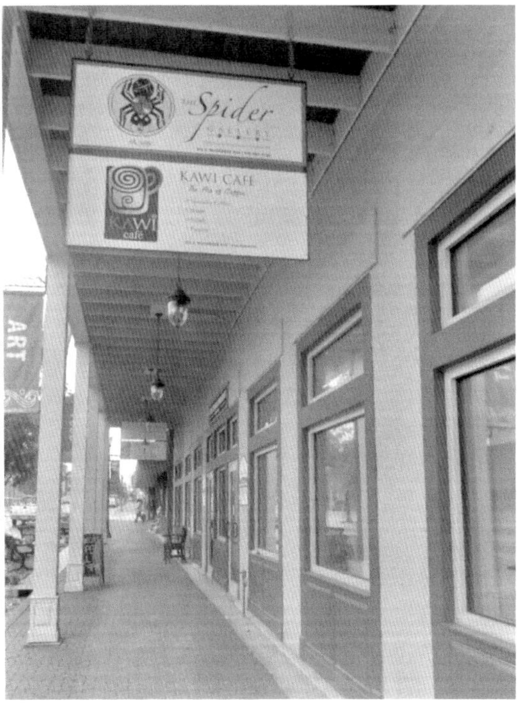

Spider Gallery in downtown Tahlequah is one of many sales outlets available to Cherokee basket makers today. *Karen Coody Cooper.*

Spider Gallery opened in 2013 with an array of attractive display windows in Tahlequah's historic downtown area. The gallery, in conjunction with the Cherokee Arts Center, hosts a website for Cherokee artists, offers studio space, prints and distributes individual artist information cards and sponsors craft and business classes with an available wide array of tools and supplies; workshop fees are fully retained by instructors. The center is housed in handsomely refurbished historic buildings and includes the popular Kawi Café (a food services training site). The center

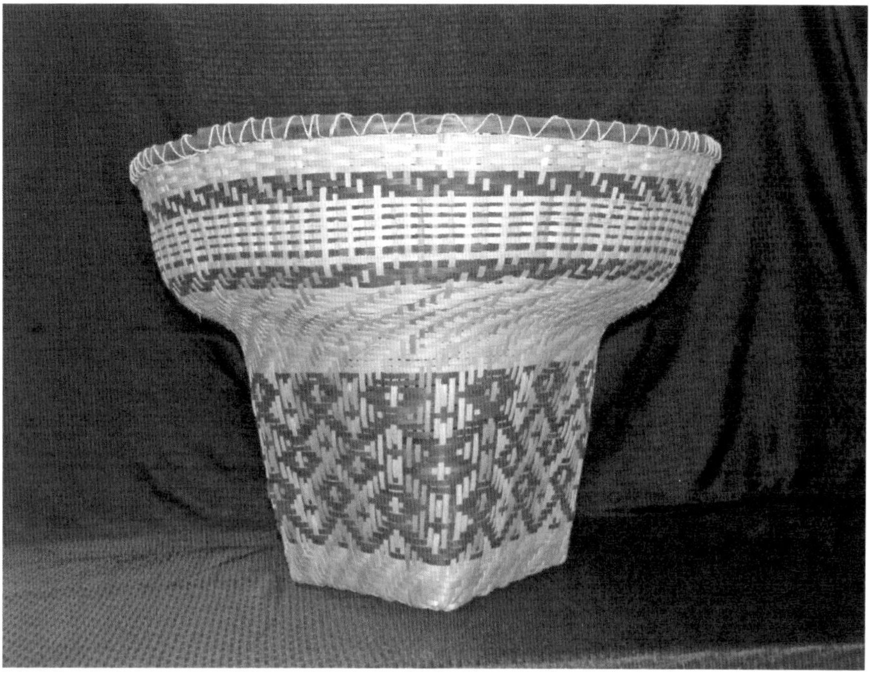

Mike Dart named his contemporary Cherokee wood splint burden basket "The Burdens We Carry." *Lisa Rutherford.*

works hard to connect artists to audiences and sales opportunities, as well as providing them with business training and assistance. If anyone is looking to interview a Cherokee artist or seek private lessons from one, the center can effectively handle such inquiries. Further, the center serves all Tahlequah area residents by inviting non-Cherokee artists to hold short-duration, small exhibits in the pass-through gallery, and it hosts and manages events important to the community at large. Donna Tinnin, community tourism director at Cherokee Nation Enterprises, manages not only the Cherokee Arts Center and Spider Gallery but also the well-attended Labor Day weekend Cherokee National Holiday festivities, as well as an annual town-wide festival for all artists. She repeatedly advises community leaders and the artists she serves that a rising tide floats all boats. The community of Tahlequah is currently benefiting from Cherokee successes, and vice versa, encouraging cooperation from all sectors.

The Southeast Indian Artists Association (SEIAA, formerly the Cherokee Artists Association) is an active Native American not-for-profit organization providing another website for artist members to post their work. The group meets monthly at the Cherokee Arts Center. Basket makers lacking funds to sign up for tables at art shows and festivals can, for a small annual membership fee, share table space with SEIAA members. Additionally, the organization has been instrumental in creating group shows involving its members. Meetings provide a forum for artists to discuss their work and develop important professional links.

To attract public attention to its 2012 exhibition, "Cherokee Baskets—History Woven in Art," the Cherokee Heritage Center tapped the talents of two young basket makers, Rachel Dew and Donnay Leach, to create "The World's Tallest Cherokee Basket," an 8-foot-high, forty-five-inch square-based woven container made of 3,300 feet of commercial smoked reed brightened with commercial dyes. Employing traditional designs such as Double Chief's Daughter and Bird's Eye View of Lightning, plus a third band combining Mountains, Crosses and Clover, the giant basket brought

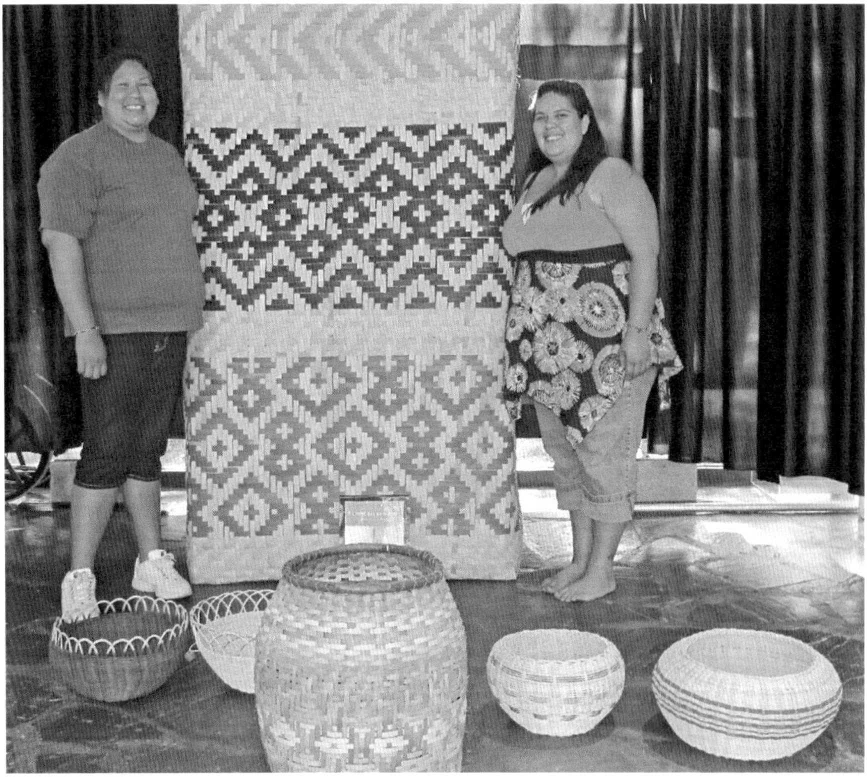

Rachel Dew, *right*, and Donnay Leach designed and wove an eight-foot-tall Cherokee basket to promote a 2012 basketry exhibition. *Cherokee National Historical Society.*

new attention to Oklahoma Cherokee basketry.[201] Basket makers discussed in the exhibition text included Lena Blackbird, Shawna Morton Cain, Rose Chewie, Mary Foreman, Thelma Forrest, Betty Frogg, Betty Garner, Cindy Hair, Anna Sixkiller Huckaby, Kathryn Kelley, Eunice O'Field, Marie Proctor, Bessie Russell, Kathy Van Buskirk and Nadine Wilbourn.[202] An upcoming exhibit will focus on Living Treasures, and some of the basket makers' works will be honored again, helping keep their work before the eyes of collectors, historians and aspiring basket makers.

Between the Cherokee Nation Gift Shop at tribal headquarters and the Cherokee Heritage Center's museum store (not the only Cherokee-managed gift shops in the area), the works of the following seventeen basket makers were available to the public in 2014: Darlene Crosby, Lela Cummings, Shirley Budder, Mike Dart, Joan Foreman, Marcella Foreman, Thelma Forrest, Kendall McCoy, Sandra Pallie, Bessie Russell, Teresa Million, Regina Thompson, Louisa Soap, Lena Stick, Loretta Bradford, Lisa Forrest and Charlotte Coats.[203] Half of the basket makers are resident in the region surrounding Kenwood, and half do not routinely enter their work in art shows. The fact that half the members of the group have won prizes says the rest produce similar quality but are not interested in competing. The hoopla of awards and application processes is understandably not appealing to everyone, plus the effort of submitting to shows can be time consuming with paperwork, delivery and pickup factors. However, one doesn't have to win prizes to make good baskets or to find buyers for them.

For example, two descendants of renowned Cherokee basket makers—unnoted in newspapers, unfound on vendor lists, unrewarded by awards—set up sales tables during the 2014 Cherokee National Holiday market held at the CHC. Loretta Buffington, daughter of Eunice O'Field, and Billie Joe Sapp, son of Jennie Sapp, talked about their work and their mothers. For the current generation, basket income is welcome money, enriching their quality of life, plus it continues family traditions.

The biggest current influence on Oklahoma Cherokee arts, including basketry, is the influx of currency from casino operations. That money supports education, health services, housing projects and programs like the CAC. The funds make possible an array of sales outlets, sponsor art shows within the Cherokee Nation, provide prize monies for art shows in other venues and underwrite infrastructure throughout the area. In 2014 alone, Cherokee tribal enterprises spent $300,000 purchasing Cherokee-made art. Cherokee Nation's construction budgets allot a percentage of funds to purchase arts and crafts to enhance new construction.[204] The Cherokee

Nation also now operates the Oklahoma Visitor Centers within the Cherokee jurisdiction, and Cherokee arts and crafts appear in those venues on turnpikes and interstates crisscrossing Cherokee boundaries. Cherokee Nation enhancement of local economies translates into jobs, increased personal incomes and the ability of Cherokee citizens themselves to become active purchasers of Cherokee arts and crafts.

Addressing the issue of materials used in baskets, most Cherokee competitions now include two categories: traditional and contemporary. This strategy ensures there will always be basket makers who will gather and process natural materials, as well as replicate and teach earlier basketry techniques, and there will also be basket makers who are encouraged to innovate with contemporary motifs and have the option of using nontraditional commercial weaving products if that suits their style.

Often in the world of art there are crossover crafts that are hard to pigeonhole, causing art show planners to make an effort to construct descriptions of categories in ways that won't wind up excluding inspiring innovations. The basketwork of Shan Goshorn is an example. Goshorn is enrolled with the Eastern Band of Cherokee Indians, but happenstance finds her living in Tulsa, and so her work is mentioned in this book. Her baskets are not made of cane, nor are they made of buckbrush. She works with archival paper staves. The reason she works with paper is that she reproduces old photographs of tribal people (or copies of old documents or lists of native words or names) on sturdy paper and then cuts the paper into weaving elements. She then interlaces them in traditional styles of Cherokee baskets, carefully assembling them so the photo images rejoin into a woven image or images intersecting with other images.

"I am a multimedia artist who addresses political issues affecting Indian people today," she says.[205] Her increasingly complicated works are shown worldwide, and she regularly enters shows and has been selected for exhibitions focused entirely on her works. Her career keeps growing as her creative genius finds new modes to deliver significant messages.[206] In 2015, Goshorn was cited as a USA Distinguished Fellow in the field of traditional arts and awarded $50,000 to support her ongoing historical research and the ensuing works she weaves.[207]

A fine arts gallery in Tulsa recently posted online five Oklahoma Cherokee baskets priced from $125 to $1,500. Spider Gallery in Tahlequah displayed in its gallery at the same time twenty-two baskets ranging from $15 to $1,140. Occasionally, a masterpiece at a show can sell for $3,000 or more.[208]

Today, an ambitious and proficient Oklahoma Cherokee basket maker, even if not employed in the CHC living history village, can make a living as a basket maker. That person will work very hard, perhaps as a repeated workshop instructor; win prize money and sell art show entries; gain contracts for original pieces of work to enhance new Cherokee constructions; sell through a variety of area gift shops and online sites; obtain grants; receive honoraria for demonstrating basketry; provide a lecture or demonstration for a fee; and gain a residency at a museum or university, and thus make a living.

Generally, the more prizes one wins, the higher one's products can be priced. However, winning prizes is never a guarantee even if your work excels, and high-priced sales may not continue as trends change. One year a person can win at every art show and sell an entire inventory, and the next year she might take no prizes and find no buyers at the shows. Independent artists' incomes are not accompanied with benefits, and there are expenses that diminish or sometimes overcome profits. Basket making is currently, at best, an income supplement for most Oklahoma Cherokee basket makers. Only a few can wrestle a livelihood from basket making. Consequently, most contemporary basket makers have full-time or part-time jobs, survive on retirement income or rely on others to contribute to household support. The fate of a basket maker has the same odds of success as that of any aspiring artist. No one knows the outcome of pursuing one's passion beforehand. But there is certainly a stronger likelihood of success when many doors are open and possibilities are higher than they have been in past years.

CONCLUSION

In earliest times, Cherokee baskets had not been viewed as commercial items, although basket trade occurred between tribes before European arrival. Commerce developed and expanded as area populations grew following colonization. Cherokee Removal to Indian Territory meant a new environment and new materials for harvesting and the hardship of rebuilding farms and homes. Baskets had long served in Cherokee cooking processes and as storage containers. As prosperity grew, industrial items replaced the need for workbaskets, and basketry work transformed into making decorative household objects. The Allotment Act scattered families and limited access to natural resources while formal schooling limited intergenerational exchanges of traditional information. Statehood ended Cherokee governmental autonomy followed by extensive Cherokee property losses for dams and lakes and recreational areas, for military use and for state and county governmental functions. Constant disruption kept most Oklahoma Cherokee citizens from experiencing stability. Festivals and fairs led to competitions and opportunities, and economic revival efforts led to more opportunities. Eventually, some basketry forms qualified as art objects. As time passed, baskets became a multitude of different things to different citizens: a means of income while staying at home, continuation of traditional values and activities, a fulfilling leisure activity, gratification for one's ego and/or a challenge to master new/old skills. Once upon a time, it had been easy to agree about what a Cherokee basket was. Today, there is no agreement about what an Oklahoma

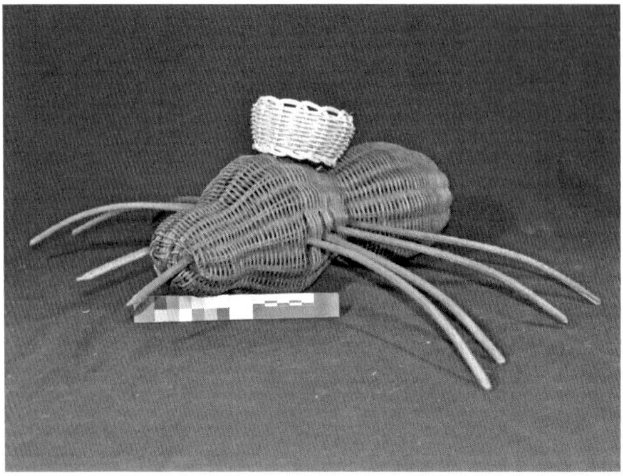

Kathy Van Buskirk, Cherokee National Living Treasure, made this spider basket to portray the legend of water spider bringing fire for warmth and light. *Cherokee National Historical Society.*

Cherokee basket is, or should be, other than it is to be made by an enrolled Cherokee citizen. Anyone not on the rosters of a federally acknowledged Cherokee government cannot legally claim to be a Cherokee Indian in the marketplace. There are currently more successful sales outlets available to Oklahoma Cherokee craftspeople, which leads to more basket production, and basket makers are more highly valued as artists today, as well as being appreciated as sustainers of Cherokee culture.

Vital to Cherokee culture are legends, the stories of the beginnings of a people, and there are many talented storytellers in the Cherokee Nation. An oft-repeated tale concerning baskets (or pottery in some versions) describes water spider weaving a basket to carry an ember of fire retrieved in a dangerous expedition. She risked her life and used her talents to bring our world out of darkness.[209] The story is about the smallest of us being capable of efforts of huge import and reminds us to be thankful for heat and light, which allow our families to live in comfort.

This symbolism is powerful. Baskets have been venerated for generations, had once been made for ceremonial uses and are seen as a tool of enlightenment and advancement. Cherokee basket makers value the cultural role their craft plays within Cherokee traditions. Oklahoma Cherokee basketry is no longer a threatened art; instead, it continues again as a mainstay of Cherokee culture, and once again, most Cherokee homes contain an impressive Cherokee basket or two or more, reminiscent of the earliest Cherokee practices.

LIST OF EARLY OKLAHOMA CHEROKEE BASKET MAKERS

(BORN 1930 OR EARLIER)

In the case of multiple generations, the eldest ancestor is noted as 1, the next generation of that family as 2 and a third generation as 3. A single generation entry has no number. The following information was derived from Ancestry.com, various census records, Find a Grave and other cemetery records, Dawes Roll, family postings, obituaries, Social Security Death Index and comments from various noted materials. Errors may occur (even census records and tombstones are not always accurate). This is not a complete list; almost all the following people were noted in a historical record.

1. **Elsie Wickliffe Backwater** (1892–?), Salina. Taught her daughter how to make baskets.[210]
2. **Ella Mae Backwater Blackbear** (1930–1991), Salina. Buckbrush. Learned to make baskets by watching her mother. The subject of the 1982 video *Cherokee Basketmaker*, Blackbear was known for baby cradles. A 1978 basket is owned by the Museum of the Red River and shown in *Basketry of Southeastern Indians*.[211] A lidded basket traveled with the 1986–88 national exhibition "Lost and Found Traditions," plus a basket took first prize in the Gallup Ceremonial.[212] She was selected in 1990 as a Cherokee National Living Treasure. A lidded buckbrush basket and a cradle are pictured in *Cherokee Quarterly*,[213] while a double-weave buckbrush basket, purchased by the Cherokee Casino Resort, appears in *Building One Fire*.[214]

1. **Lizzy Backwater** (circa 1870–?), Eucha. Headed a family of basket makers.
2. **Katie Backwater Proctor** (1895–1982), Kenwood. Buckbrush. Sold baskets to Oklahoma Office of Indian Affairs for resale and taught her daughters basket making.[215]
2. **Eliza Backwater Proctor** (circa 1900–2000), Kenwood. Buckbrush. Photo posted on Eliza Proctor's Steeley Cemetery Find A Grave website shows her with two large handsome baskets at her feet while weaving another.[216] She's listed on a Field Service sales list as selling ten baskets, more than any other on the list for that accounting period.[217]
3. **Celia (Cecile) Proctor Littledeer** (1915–1975), Cookson Hills. She sold baskets through the Tahlequah Weaver's sales outlet. *Tulsa World Reporter* Quinlan wrote that Little Deer was "the Cookson Hills' basket making champion."[218] Listed by Marriott.[219]
3. **Jennie Proctor Sapp** (1923–1995), Jay/Kenwood/Salina. Buckbrush double-weave. Williamson Museum in Louisiana shows a basket from its collection in its catalogue *The Old Ways Live*.[220] She became a teacher of the craft[221] and was named in 1990 as a National Living Treasure. She was noted in *Cherokee Quarterly*'s 2000 issue.[222] Lost Arts Project cited her baskets as being in the collections of the Smithsonian and the Heard Museum.[223] She was a Bull Hollow Weavers member, and one of her baskets is maintained by the Delaware County Historical Society in Jay, Oklahoma.
3. **Marie Proctor** (circa 1926–?), Kenwood. Buckbrush and honeysuckle with natural dyes. In 2006, she was named Keetoowah Tradition Keeper.[224] One of her baskets was exhibited in the Cherokee Heritage Center exhibition "Cherokee Baskets—History Woven in Art" in 2012. Retired Gilcrease curator noted her in *Cherokee Quarterly*'s 2000 issue.[225]

Mary Mouse Bark (circa 1903–1980), Delaware County. Buckbrush. Listed in ledger of Sequoyah Weavers.[226]

Mary Bigacorn (1914–?), Kenwood. Sold baskets for resale to Oklahoma Office of Indian Affairs Field Service.[227]

Rachel Bird (circa 1870–?), Salina. Cane. Noted in *Tulsa World*, September 8, 1940, as working on bundles of cane in preparation for basket making.[228]

Mary Polly Blackfox (circa 1900–), Salina. Buckbrush. A basket of hers is owned by Ken Masters, inherited from his grandmother Maud Peak, who received it as payment for midwife services.[229]

Rabbit (1897–1945) and **Bessie Boney** (1907–1963), Kenwood. Buckbrush. Both sold baskets to Field Service for resale.[230]

Lucy and Cullis Buck (circa 1910–?), Kenwood/Eucha. Buckbrush. Alice Marriott noted that Cullis Buck "is one of the finest of the Cherokee basket makers." Cullis was recommended by Marriott as a teacher of basketry to a Civilian Conservation Corps group in Kenwood, and the couple demonstrated basketry at the Tulsa Fair. Steve, Henry, Homer and Jennie Buck also made baskets in Kenwood.[231] A photo of Lucy Buck with a basket started is in the Wilburn Cartwright Photograph Collection at Oklahoma University.[232]

Jennie Buckskin (1896–1978), Salina/Kenwood. Buckbrush. Member of Bull Hollow, pictured on "Cherokee Images" website.[233]

1. **Aggie Mouse Budder** (1902–1980), Eucha/Jay. Buckbrush. She taught her daughters to weave. Her large clothes hamper, a round hand basket and a market basket appear in *Cherokee Quarterly*.[234] Cited by Marriott as a Kenwood basket maker.[235]
2. **Maxine Budder Stick** (1931–2004), Eucha/Jay. Buckbrush. Learned from her mother, Aggie Budder. Made double-wall baskets, sometimes with handles and/or lids, and was especially known for her clothes hampers and market baskets. Photo of circular basket tray appears in *Basketry of the Southeastern Indians*[236] and is in the collection of the Museum of the Red River. She has four baskets in the National Museum of the American Indian collections (259089.000, 259091.000, 259096.000 and 263834.000).[237] She took first prize in 2004 in the Trail of Tears Art Show and is noted in *Cherokee Quarterly*'s 2000 issue. One of her buckbrush baskets was presented to President Ronald Reagan and subsequently placed in the National Archives.[238] She co-founded the Kenwood Arts and Crafts Cooperative in 1988 and was named a Cherokee National Living Treasure in 1990.[239]

1. **Ollie Budder** (1895–?), Kenwood. Sold baskets to Field Service.[240]
2. **Annie Budder** (1913–). Noted as a basket maker by Marriott.[241]

Squirrel Croslin (1921–?). Participated in Haskell Indian Arts Market.[242] Won second prize in Art Under the Oaks in Muskogee, Oklahoma, in 1996.

Sanford Cummings (1930–1995), Tahlequah. His basket hat, shown in *Basketry of Southeastern Indians*,[243] is in the collections of the Museum of the Red River. He also produced animal shapes.

1. **Hattie Leach Downing** (1902–1982), Bryan. Buckbrush. Her daughter remembers Downing boiling buckbrush outside in a kettle.[244]
2. **Mary L. Downing Foreman** (1926–2000), Oaks. Preferred honeysuckle. Instructed by Thelma Forrest, although her own mother was a basket maker. Quoted in *Southeastern Native Arts Directory*.[245] One of six basket makers selected in 1990 as a Living National Treasure. Quoted in *Mid-America Folklore*, 1988.[246] Her honeysuckle basket, Footsteps on the Trail of Tears, appears in *Cherokee Quarterly*.[247] One of her honeysuckle baskets is in the collections of the National Museum of the American Indian (254617.000),[248] and some of her baskets traveled to Germany. She collected awards at Five Civilized Tribes Museum and art shows in Cherokee Nation. One of her baskets was in the Cherokee Heritage Center exhibition "Cherokee Baskets—History Woven in Art" in 2012. She taught classes at Oaks, Rocky Ford, Tahlequah, Kenwood and schools in the area.

1. **Ollie (A-li) Duck** (circa 1840–?). Came to Indian Territory as a Cherokee émigré from Georgia. Her grandson George Duck recalled in an Indian-Pioneer Papers interview that she borrowed cash from a neighbor and then paid the debt with baskets she made.[249]
2. **Lucy Duck** (circa 1860–?), Adair County. Lucy and her mother, Ollie, regularly sold baskets to people in the Evansville, Arkansas area.[250]

Betty Scraper Garner (1924–1997). Named a National Living Treasure in 1993.[251] One of her baskets was chosen to be in the Cherokee Heritage Center exhibition "Cherokee Baskets—History Woven in Art" in 2012. In 2014, the Cherokee Heritage Center gave her the Cherokee Elder Artist Award.

Lula Scraper Gibbons (1901–1983), Baron. Buckbrush. Hosted workshops at her home. Sold baskets at the Muskogee Fair.[252] Noted in *Cherokee Quarterly* 2000 issue as teaching basketry.[253]

ALICE GUESS GLORY (1925–2001), Jay. Noted in *Cherokee Quarterly*.[254]

SUSAN (SUSE) HIDER SOLDIER GLORY (1873–?), Kenwood/Eucha. She had two baskets in the Philbrook Field Collection: a sifter made in 1937 (1948.39.54) and a basket with handle in 1940 (1948.39.168).[255] Alice Marriott, of the Indian Arts and Crafts Board's Oklahoma City office, wrote that members of the Soldier family "make very good baskets."[256] Susan had been a student at the Cherokee Female Seminary.[257]

ANNIE HAIR (circa 1900–?), Round Springs. Buckbrush. Reported to produce one hundred baskets per year for an income of forty dollars; she noted that if she could find a strong market, she would make two hundred a year.[258]

ELIZA C. HAIR (1883–1963), Kenwood/Jay/Eucha. Sold baskets to Field Service.[259] Referenced as Mrs. Dave Hair.[260]

EFFIE JONES (1911–2000), Jay/Grove. Honeysuckle. Listed in *Cherokee Quarterly* as a basket maker.[261] Remembered as a member of the Jay Weavers. Photo on website of "Cherokee Images."[262]

FANNIE THOMPSON JUMPER (1881–?), Oaks/Jay. Buckbrush. Her husband's given name was Pleasant/Plez. She made a wicker-plaited buckbrush rectangular shallow basket, circa 1941, collected by Field, now at Philbrook (1948.39.204).[263] She is mentioned in a *Tulsa World* article.[264] The Delaware County Historical Society in Jay, Oklahoma, maintains five of her baskets.[265] The 1941 annual report of the Five Civilized Tribes extension office said that Jumper "is the outstanding basket maker among the Cherokees" and notes that she was both a teacher and demonstrator at the Anadarko Fair and state fairs at Muskogee and Oklahoma State University.[266]

MILDRED JUSTICE KETCHER (1922–1983). Named a National Treasure posthumously in 1999.[267] She married John Ketcher, who helped start Tahlequah Weavers. She traveled to North Carolina with Thelma Forrest to research basketry.[268]

1. **ANNA E. CHRISTIE LANGLEY** (1902–?), Christie. Taught her daughter the basics of basket weaving.
2. **MAVIS DOERING** (1929–2007), Hominy/Oklahoma City. Buckbrush woven with commercial flat reed. She learned the basics from her mother

and then took classes at Cherokee Nation.[269] Her husband aided in gathering and preparing basketry materials. She participated in thirteen Santa Fe Indian Markets. A double-wall buckbrush and ash splint basket is in the collections of the National Museum of the American Indian (254790.000), and one is in the Five Civilized Tribes Museum collections (93.1.1.B).

STELLA LIVERS (1910–1993), Stilwell. Buckbrush. She taught basketry in her home.[270] She entered a basket in a Philbrook competition in 1969.[271] *Muskogee Phoenix* wrote about her work on April 4, 1985. Noted in *Mid-America Folklore* as one of the master basket makers in the area.[272] One of six basket makers named in 1990 as a National Living Treasure.[273]

LUCY MOUSE (1902–?), Salina/Kenwood. Buckbrush. Clark Field noted that Mouse produced a strong, durable basket.[274] One of her baskets, collected by Field, is now at Philbrook Museum (1942.14.1920)[275] and pictured in *Smithsonian Handbook of North American Indians*, Southeast Volume.[276] Two examples (2-1464 and 2-1465) are in the collections of the Burke Museum in Seattle. A photo of a double-weave buckbrush basket illustrates "Root Runner Baskets in Oklahoma."[277] A demonstration basket by Mouse showing the double weave partly done was obtained by Clark Field in 1930 and donated to the anthropology collections of the National Museum of Natural History, Smithsonian (241754). A fine example of a tightly woven double-wall buckbrush wastebasket is in the Five Civilized Tribes Museum collections (1964.72.01).

MINNIE MOUSE (1892–1968), Jay/Kenwood. Noted as a basket maker in a *Tulsa World* article.[278] Sold baskets to Field Service office.[279]

ANNIE OOSAWEE (Oosahwe) (1872–after 1930), Jay. Cane. Her brother Taylor L. Harry noted that he gathered cane for two of his sisters who made riddles from them.[280]

JENNIE SAPSUCKER OWENS (1894–1975), Salina. Buckbrush. She married Judge Owens (a given name, not a title). A collected buckbrush basket in the author's private collection has its Sequoyah Weavers tag attached with Jennie Owens named as the basket maker.

Millie Pigeon (circa 1857–1938), Cookson. Cane. It was reported in a 1930s interview that she presently had cane split and drying on her porch and sold baskets to make a living.[281] Her mother was Annie Christie, born in Georgia before the Removal, and she likely taught her daughter to weave.

Minnie Potter (circa 1898–?). A photo and caption appeared in *Tulsa World* of her preparing buckbrush for basketry.[282]

1. **Josie Proctor** (1899–1972), Kenwood. Buckbrush. She washed gathered material in the creek to prepare it for weaving, noted her daughter Maggie.[283]
2. **Maggie Proctor Alberty** (1928–1997), Kenwood/Tulsa. Buckbrush. Born into a family of basket makers, Maggie started making baskets at six years old. After marriage and moving to Tulsa, she abandoned the craft for a period and then resumed again.[284] Her work is mentioned in *Mid-America Folklore*[285] and has been displayed at Gilcrease and Philbrook.

Sallie Proctor (?). Listed by Marriott.[286]

1. **Jennie Wickliffe Raper** (1898–1995), Salina/Kenwood. Her daughter remembered her as being a basket maker.
3. **Eunice O'Field** (1934–2002), Kenwood. Split willow, buckbrush, hickory. Made workbaskets as well as pretty baskets. In 1992, she was designated a National Living Treasure. Her work appears in the collection of the Williamson Museum in Louisiana and in its catalogue book *The Old Ways Live*.[287] Her 1983 sifter of split willow is pictured in *Cherokee Quarterly*.[288] A photo of O'Field working on a basket appears in the Smithsonian's Southeast Volume 14, *Handbook of North American Indians*.[289] Her work was shown in the Cherokee Heritage Center exhibition "Cherokee Baskets—History Woven in Art" in 2012. The Gettys collection has two examples, one being a wood sifter made in 2005 and the other a buckbrush bowl made in 2001.

Elsie (Ella) Redbird (1870–1955), Kenwood/Jay/Eucha. Sold baskets to Field Service, Office of Indian Affairs, in Oklahoma City.[290]

1. **Susie Redbird** (1902–?). Appears on a list of basket makers selling through Field Service.[291]
2. **Sally Redbird Lacy** (1920–1990), Kenwood/Salina. Buckbrush. Made double-weave as well as wicker-plaited baskets as early as 1935. Large

storage basket made in 1941 used as illustration in *Art of the Cherokee*,[292] and a buckbrush hamper is in *Woven Worlds*.[293] She is found in a ledger book of Sequoyah Weavers and was one of six basket makers named National Living Treasures in 1990. Two baskets are in Philbrook's Field Collection: double-wall buckbrush striped basket with lid and handles (1948.39.173) and double-wall storage basket (1948.39.67). One basket is in the Spencer Museum of Art in Lawrence, Kansas.

Arlie Reeves (1867–?), Webbers Falls. Hickory, buckbrush.[294]

1. **Susan Sawney** (1864–?), Lees Creek, Adair County.
2. **Lydia Sawney Adair** (1894–?), Bunch. Buckbrush. Won second prize for a flower basket at the 1944 Oklahoma State Fair in Muskogee.[295]
2. **Annie Sawney Jones** (1901–?), Bunch. Buckbrush. Won first prize for a basket at the 1944 Oklahoma State Fair in Muskogee.[296]

Diana Scott (1905–1997). Made baskets in CHC Ancient Village. Taught Lena Blackbird.[297]

1. **Winnie Blackwood Sixkiller** (1844–1929). Born in North Carolina. Taught her daughters basket weaving. She only spoke Cherokee.
2. **Eliza Jane Sixkiller Padgett** (1870–1950), Stilwell, Wauhilla. Two of her baskets were collected by Clark Field: wicker-plaited storage basket in 1937[298] and buckbrush basket featuring openwork lattice with braided rim base in 1930. The Five Civilized Tribes Museum[299] and Oklahoma Historical Society each collected a piece. One of her buckbrush baskets is shown in the Smithsonian's Southeast Volume 14, *Handbook of North American Indians*.[300]
2. **Mary Sixkiller Muskrat** (1874–?). Married to John Muskrat. Recorded as a weaver.
2. **Ora Sixkiller Watt Hogner** (1881–?). Husband was William Hogner.
2. **Nannie/Nancy Sixkiller Hogner** (1883–1940), Eucha. Early basket maker and teacher of the craft. There is an archived photo of several displayed baskets during a teaching session at the Indian women's club of Claremore.[301] One of her baskets, collected by Clark Field, is in the Philbrook Collection.[302]

Donna Spade (circa 1880–?), Kenwood. Made in 1900 a wicker-plaited oak basket with bent wood handle that appears in Field Collection at Philbrook[303] and appears in the Smithsonian's *Handbook of North American Indians*.[304]

Maggie Spade (1891–?). Worked with buckbrush, honeysuckle and white oak, according to granddaughter Anna Sixkiller, in a personal interview with the author in 2014.

Pollie Spade (1904–1985), Kenwood. Sold baskets to Field Service.[305]

Jennie Studie (1919–?). Appears in a 1940 photo of women working on buckbrush materials.[306]

1. **Nancy Proctor Tanner** (1885–?), Eucha/Kenwood. Noted that her top-selling week, a record in the area, was $3.50.[307] Her name is on the Marriott accounting list.[308]
2. **Fanny Tanner** (?), Eucha. Listed by Marriott.[309]
2. **Sallie Tanner Soldier** (1911–?), Kenwood. Listed by Marriott.[310]
2. **Rachel Tanner Davis** (1924–?). Known for producing a diamond pattern.[311] Her photo is in the Wilburn Cartwright photograph collection.[312] Her name is on the Marriott list.

Nellie Tucker (1914–2005), Chewey/Oaks. Made double-weave buckbrush baskets in the 1950s. Noted in *Art of the Cherokee: Prehistory to Present*.[313]

Martha Vann (1900–?), Salina. Noted in a 1940 newspaper story on Cherokee basket making.[314]

Susie Bark Washington (1908–?), Salina/Hickory Ground. Reported on gathering buckbrush and making baskets for egg gathering, sewing baskets and flower containers. She sold small baskets for a quarter in 1937.[315]

Lucy Weeley (1909–1976), Eucha/Kenwood. Buckbrush. Has a basket in the collection of the National Museum of the American Indian, purchased from Oak Hill Weavers in 1965 by the Indian Arts and Craft Board for $1.25.[316] Recently, a small handled basket of hers sold on eBay with a tag noting her name, the original $2.00 price and "Oklahoma Cherokee Indian Arts & Crafts Center, Tahlequah."

Nancy Wildcat (1913–1995), Gore. Cane. Three examples are in the Philbrook Collection: a twill-plaited cane basket with handles, a cane sifter and a cane catch basket, all collected in 1941 by Clark Field.[317]

Lucy Spade Wolf (circa 1900–?), Kansas. Buckbrush. Philbrook Museum of Art possesses a double-wall tray; a round basket with a handle and blue stripe; a double-wall with handle, brown, orange, dark blue; a storage basket with two handles covered by a lid with handle; and a basket with lid and handles, all collected in 1940 as part of the Field Collection.[318]

Josephine Wolfe (1920–1988?), Westville. Noted in *Cherokee Quarterly*.[319]

Sadie Wolfe (?), Kenwood. She sold inexpensive baskets to Field Service for resale.[320]

NOTEWORTHY COLLECTIONS OF OKLAHOMA CHEROKEE BASKETS

More than five hundred Oklahoma Cherokee baskets are found in the following collections.

Bacone College, Ataloa Lodge, Muskogee, Oklahoma. Six baskets. One attributed to JOYCE JOHNSON and another to MAVIS DOERING. An old buckbrush sewing basket is circa Trail of Tears era.

Ballenger Library, Special Collections (upstairs), Northeastern State University, Tahlequah, Oklahoma. Seven baskets. Four are contemporary, and three older baskets are unidentified by maker. One was donated by Mr. and Mrs. Grant Foreman, and a copy of Foreman's 1948 basket book may be seen here.

Cherokee Heritage Center, Cherokee National Historical Society, Park Hill/Tahlequah, Oklahoma. This private nonprofit museum holds over two hundred Oklahoma Cherokee baskets, ranging from old to contemporary. Includes works of historical basket makers SUSAN SOLDIER, MRS. MOUSE and SALLY LACY.

Cherokee Nation Business (casinos and associated entities), Catoosa and Tahlequah, Oklahoma. Owns eighty-five contemporary baskets, most displayed in casino properties, medical centers and Cherokee Nation offices.

Delaware County Historical Society, Jay, Oklahoma. The museum possesses a total of seven baskets, with five made by FANNIE JUMPER, one by JENNIE SAPP and an old kanuche basket used long term by the Snell family of Jay.

Five Civilized Tribes Museum, Muskogee, Oklahoma. The museum has fourteen early twentieth-century buckbrush baskets, with one each made by LUCY MOUSE and ELIZA PADGETT. There are shopping baskets, wastebaskets, vases, bowls, plates and fruit baskets, with some unusual and well-executed designs. Two were collected and donated by Mrs. Grant Foreman (Carolyn Thomas Foreman), a Muskogee author of Oklahoma history books.

Gettys Private Collection. This collection is composed of more than eighty Oklahoma Cherokee baskets, primarily older baskets. There is a basket by LENA BLACKBIRD, two by JENNIE SAPP and two by EUNICE O'FIELD. The collection is expected to go to the Museum of the Red River in Idabel, Oklahoma.

Gilcrease Museum, Tulsa, Oklahoma. The collection consists of eleven baskets, including cane, buckbrush, hickory and commercial cane. One is attributed to JOYCE JOHNSON, three to ELLA MAE BLACKBEAR and one to MAVIS DOERING. Another is a pack basket of the 1900s.

John Hair Museum and Cultural Center, United Keetoowah Band of Cherokee, Tahlequah, Oklahoma. This center has eleven baskets, including six MARIE PROCTOR buckbrush baskets and one GEORGE FOURKILLER oak basket.

Museum of the Red River, Idabel, Oklahoma. The Oklahoma Cherokee baskets here include eight made by the following: ELLA MAE BLACKBEAR, JOYCE JOHNSON, MAVIS DOERING, SANFORD CUMMINGS, MAXINE STICK, SHIRLEY GEWIN, KATHRYN KELLEY and DANA TALBERT.

National Museum of the American Indian, Smithsonian Institution, Cultural Resources Center, Suitland, Maryland. This museum has eighteen Oklahoma Cherokee baskets: one by MARY FOREMAN, one by MAVIS DOERING, four by MAXINE STICK and two noted to have been purchased from Oak Hill Weavers with one weaver identified as LUCY WEELY (WEELEY). The Indian Arts and Crafts Board transferred its collection to NMAI. A basket made in 1930 by LUCY MOUSE is at the Smithsonian's National Museum of Natural History.

Oklahoma History Center/Oklahoma Historical Society, Oklahoma City, Oklahoma. There are eleven baskets held by the center. Being an old institution, two were collected in 1917, two in 1920 and three in 1921. Three ELIZA PADGETT baskets were collected in 1934.

Philbrook Museum of Art, Tulsa, Oklahoma. There are fifty-two baskets identified as made by Oklahoma Cherokee basket makers. Six were obtained in 2001, while the others are from the Clark Field Collection collected primarily in the 1930s and '40s. Early makers include Lucy Mouse, Lucy Spade Wolf, Eliza Padgett, Susie Soldier Glory, Sally Lacy, Nancy Sixkiller, Nancy Wildcat, Fannie Jumper and Donna Spade.

Sam Noble Oklahoma Museum of Natural History, University of Oklahoma, Norman, Oklahoma. There are six baskets related to Oklahoma Cherokee in the collection, and one is said to have come on the Trail of Tears (donated by Alice Marriott). There is a Lena Blackbird and two Joan Shoemaker baskets.

Thomas-Foreman Historic Home, a Three Rivers Museum site, is located in Muskogee, Oklahoma. About half a dozen Oklahoma Cherokee baskets are displayed as furnishings in this home of Carolyn Thomas Foreman, who wrote a volume in 1948 about Oklahoma Cherokee baskets. No makers are identified.

Williamson Museum, Northwestern State University, Natchitoches, Louisiana. Inherited the collection of Claude Medford Jr., a Choctaw basket maker and collector. Includes thirteen Oklahoma Cherokee baskets (eleven are Joyce Johnson works, and one is a Eunice O'Field cane sifter).

NOTES

Introduction

1. King and Fitzgerald, *Cherokee Trail of Tears*, 11, 70.
2. Conley, *Cherokee Encyclopedia*, 160.
3. Power, *Art of the Cherokee*, 249.
4. Mooney, *Myths of the Cherokee*, 179.
5. White, "Anthropologists and the Eastern Cherokee," 12.
6. Woodward, *Cherokees*, 7.

Cherokee Basketry Begins in the East

7. Lawson, *History of Carolina*, 189.
8. Fariello, *Cherokee Basketry*, 41.
9. Power, *Art of the Cherokee*, 57.
10. Bushnell, "Sloane Collection," 678–79.
11. Foreman, *Cherokee Weaving and Basketry*, 30–31.
12. O'Brien, "Cherokee Baskets," 21.
13. Adair, *History of the Indians*, 424.
14. Culin, *Games of the North American Indians*, 105.
15. Adair, *History of the Indians*, 424.
16. Conley, *Cherokee*, 46; Foreman, *Cherokee Weaving and Basketry*, 21, 30–31; Thornton, *Cherokees*, 44.
17. Power, *Art of the Cherokee*, 87.

18. Crews and Starbuck, *Records of the Moravians*, 1474.
19. Ibid.
20. Hill, "Weaving History," 117.
21. Ibid., 115.
22. Yale Peabody Museum of Anthropology.
23. Power, *Art of the Cherokee*, 87; Hill, "Weaving History," 129–30.
24. Duggan and Riggs, *Studies in Cherokee Basketry*, 41.
25. Ibid.

New Beginnings in the West

26. King and Fitzgerald, *Cherokee Trail of Tears*, 11.
27. Foreman, *Indian Removal*, 287.
28. Ibid., 261.
29. Morgan Friedman investment corporation, "Inflation Calculator."
30. University of Tennessee, Penelope Johnson Allen Collection.
31. McDaniel, "Vann Slaves Remember."
32. Power, *Art of the Cherokee*, 48.
33. Duggan and Riggs, *Studies in Cherokee Basketry*, 27.
34. Indian-Pioneer Papers, recorded interview with Lucinda Hickey, vol. 42.
35. Ibid., recorded interview with Rachel Dodge, vol. 25.
36. Emerson, *Houstons of Tahlequah*, 249.
37. Indian-Pioneer Papers, recorded interview with Rachel Dodge, vol. 25.
38. Wright, "American Indian Corn Dishes," 157.
39. Indian-Pioneer Papers, recorded interview with Arlie Reeves, vol. 75.
40. Ibid., recorded interview with Ellen Shanon Magee, vol. 60.
41. Buffington, conversation with author.
42. Coats, "Hamburg Cane."

Historical Baskets with Ties to East and West

43. King and Fitzgerald, *Cherokee Trail of Tears*, 70.
44. Sam Noble Museum of Natural History.
45. Burke, personal communication with curator.
46. Indian-Pioneer Papers, recorded interview with Dorothy Field Morgan, vol. 64, 3.
47. Conley, *Cherokee*, 47.

48. Timothy, Ataloa Lodge.
49. Fariello, personal communication via e-mail.
50. Native Plant Information Network.

Cherokee Basketry Evolution in the West

51. Johnson, *Cherokee Baskets*.
52. Oklahoma Department of Forestry.
53. Field, *Art and Romance of Indian Basketry*, 30.
54. Duggan and Riggs, *Studies in Cherokee Basketry*, 29.
55. Reed, "Cherokee Weaver Helps Recreate Lost Artifacts."
56. Indian-Pioneer Papers, recorded interview with Dorothy Field Morgan, vol. 64, 3; Five Civilized Tribes Museum.
57. Foreman, *Cherokee Weaving and Basketry*, 30,
58. Field, *Art and Romance of Indian Basketry*, 30.
59. Swearingen, *Cherokee Basket Maker*.
60. Sallee, "Don't Trip on the Devil's Shoestring."
61. Cain, "Buckbrush."
62. NARA.
63. Anderson, "Indians Strive to Preserve Native Art of Basketry."
64. Conley, *Cherokee Encyclopedia*, 262.
65. Field, *Art and Romance of Indian Basketry*, 30.
66. Lombardi, "Basketmaking," 9.
67. Mihesuah, *Cultivating the Rosebuds*, 31.
68. Everett, "Fairs."
69. Mullins, "Horse Races."
70. Everett, "Fairs."
71. O'Brien, "Cherokee Baskets," 15; Lombardi, "Basketmaking," 6.
72. Lombardi, "Basketmaking," 5.
73. Johnson, *Cherokee Baskets*; Bliss, *North American Dye Plants*, 18; Lemaster, "Cherokee Baskets," 24.
74. *Joplin Globe*, October 6, 1966.
75. Lombardi, "Basketmaking," 8.
76. Bliss, *North American Dye Plants*, 18.
77. Indian-Pioneer Papers, recorded interview with Millie Pigeon, vol. 71.
78. Ibid., recorded interview with George Duck, vol. 26.
79. Power, *Art of the Cherokee*, 147.
80. NARA.

81. Philbrook Museum of Art collections, record 1948.27.14.
82. Five Civilized Tribes Museum collection, record 1964.09.02.
83. Oklahoma History Center collection, records 04185, 04186 and 04187.
84. Sturtevant, *Handbook of North American Indians*, 371.
85. Philbrook Museum of Art collection, record 1948.39.162.
86. Indian-Pioneer Papers, recorded interview with Jennie Hines, vol. 42.
87. Fariello, *Cherokee Basketry*, 92.
88. Anderson, personal communication.

Allotment, Statehood and the Development of Collecting

89. Debo, *And Still the Waters Run*, 6.
90. Stremlau, *Sustaining the Cherokee Family*, 221.
91. Western History Collections, interview with Lula Hair.
92. Faulk and Jones, *Tahlequah*, 107.
93. Cherokee Heritage Center collections, record O76-200003-23NSU.
94. Duvall, *Cherokee Nation*, 54.
95. Sattler, "Baskets of the Cherokees," 29.
96. Ballenger Room.
97. Philbrook Museum of Art, records 1948.39.54 and 1948.39.168.
98. Cherokee Heritage Center, record O76-221.
99. O'Brien, "Cherokee Baskets," 16.
100. Field, *Art and Romance of Indian Basketry*, 8.
101. Starr-Scott, telephone conversation with author.
102. Anderson, "Indians Strive to Preserve Native Art of Basketry."
103. Quinlan, "Is Indian Basket Making Becoming a Lost Art?"
104. O'Brien, "Cherokee Baskets," 16.
105. Ibid.
106. Foster, presentation at Pocahontas Indian Women's Club.
107. Gettys, conversation with author.
108. Flippo, "Cherokee Baskets," 13–18.
109. Quinlan, "Is Indian Basket Making Becoming a Lost Art?"; *Tulsa World*, "Chelsea Woman Aids Cherokee Weavers."
110. Anderson, "Indians Strive to Preserve Native Art of Basketry."
111. Meredith, account of family recollections.
112. Field, *Art and Romance of Indian Basketry*, 30.
113. Wyckoff, *Woven Worlds*, 13
114. Gettys, *Southeast: Woven Worlds*, 189.

115. Wyckoff, *Woven Worlds*, 229.
116. Ibid., 23.
117. Ibid., 28–29.
118. Hill, "Marketing Traditions," 212.
119. Matt Reed, list of Oklahoma Cherokee baskets.

Poverty, Depression and Recovery Programs

120. Masters, e-mail exchanges.
121. Hill, "Marketing Traditions," 223.
122. Quinlan, "Is Indian Basket Making Becoming a Lost Art?"
123. Indian Arts and Crafts Board.
124. Laughlin, online biography of Alice Lee Marriott.
125. Marriott Papers, Box 7, File 15.
126. Ibid., Box 77, File 11.
127. Ibid., Box 15, File 5.
128. Ibid., Box 17, File 13.
129. Foreman, *Cherokee Weaving and Basketry*, 31.
130. Marriott Papers, Box 7, File 16.
131. Anderson, "Indians Strive to Preserve Native Art of Basketry."
132. Laughlin, online biography of Alice Lee Marriott.
133. Indian Arts and Crafts Board.
134. Anderson, "Indians Strive to Preserve Native Art of Basketry."
135. Lombardi, "Basketmaking," 7.
136. Ancestry.com, Oklahoma and Indian Territory.
137. Unattributed published clipping in files of author.
138. Anderson, "Indians Strive to Preserve Native Art of Basketry."
139. Indian-Pioneer Papers, recorded interview with Millie Pigeon, vol. 71, 1937.
140. NARA.
141. Cherokee Phoenix, "TCCO to Host Meeting."
142. Mankiller, profile of Ketcher.

Self-Help Struggles and Museum Growth

143. Conley, *Cherokee Encyclopedia*, 152.
144. Foreman, *Cherokee Weaving and Basketry*, 21, 30–31, 33.

145. Wright, "American Indian Corn Dishes," 157.
146. Mirro-Krome, *Indians of the Southwest.*
147. *Miami (OK) Daily News*, December 1959, 10.
148. Smithsonian Institution.
149. Sequoyah Indian Weavers, *International Textile Exposition*.
150. Victory Papers.
151. Foreman, *Cherokee Weaving and Basketry*, 21.
152. Victory Papers; Morgan Friedman investment corporation, "Inflation Calculator."
153. Murphy, "Sequoyah Indian Weavers Hall Needs Makeover."
154. Victory Papers.
155. National Museum of the American Indian.
156. Morgan Friedman investment corporation, "Inflation Calculator."
157. *New Castle (PA) News*, October 27, 1969.
158. *Joplin (MO) Globe*, June 1, 1971.
159. Five Civilized Tribes Museum.
160. Cherokee Nation.
161. CN files.
162. *Stilwell (OK) Democrat-Journal*, April 25, 1960, 2.
163. Indian Education Hearings.
164. *Stilwell (OK) Democrat-Journal*, February 15, 1968, 4.
165. Ibid., 1973.
166. Cherokee Heritage Center.
167. Cherokee National Treasures.

Art Shows and Exhibitions Develop

168. Wyckoff, *Woven Worlds*, 29.
169. Ibid.
170. Fredrick, "Cherokee Baskets of Oklahoma Origin"; Chavez, "Cherokee Basket Maker Shares Her Talent."
171. Sattler, "Baskets of the Cherokees," 32.
172. Turnbaugh and Turnbaugh, *Indian Baskets*, 98.
173. Ibid., 106.
174. Ibid., 100.

Recognition of Oklahoma Cherokee Baskets

175. Coe, *Lost and Found Traditions*, 85.
176. Klein, "Kenwood Artisans."
177. Devlin, *Oklahoma Today*, 5.
178 Cherokee National Treasures.
179. Lost Arts Project booklet.
180. Power, *Art of the Cherokee*, 209.
181. Klein, "Kenwood Artisans."
182. National Museum of the American Indian.
183. Klein, "Kenwood Artisans."
184. Ibid.
185. Chumwalooky, interview with author.
186. Foster, provided a tour; Chumwalooky, interview with author.
187. Gregory, *Old Ways Live*, 91, 95, 96.
188. Agard-Smith, *Southeastern Native Arts Directory*, 102, 104–5, 108.

Contemporary Cherokee Basketry Issues

189. Ataloa, "Revival of Indian Art."
190. Sattler, "Baskets of the Cherokees," 32.
191. Wicker Woman.
192. Coats, "Hamburg Cane."
193. Cottrell, www.basketsbyviv.wix.com.
194. Chavez, "Cottrell Carries On."
195. Cottrell, www.basketsbyviv.wix.com.
196. Devlin, *Oklahoma Today*, 23.

The New Millennium and Casino Cash

197. Holiday, song lyric.
198. Gettys, *Southeast: Woven Worlds*, 189.
199. Wyckoff, *Woven Worlds*, 225–26.
200. Power, *Art of the Cherokee*, 206–8.
201. *Cherokee Phoenix*, "World's Tallest Cherokee Basket."
202. Craig, "Cherokee Heritage Center," 1.
203. Taylor, e-mail sent to author; Roastingear, e-mail sent to author.

204. CN press release, August 2014.
205. Goshorn, *Shan Goshorn Studio.*
206. Watts, "Basket Beauty," D3.
207. Watts, "Tulsan Shan Goshorn Earns Fellowship Honor," D2.
208. Author survey of prices in shops and online, 2015.

Conclusion

209. Mooney, *Myths of the Cherokee*, 241.

List of Early Oklahoma Cherokee Basket Makers

210. Klein, "Kenwood Artisans."
211. Sattler, "Baskets of the Cherokees."
212. Coe, *Lost and Found Traditions*, 85.
213. Flippo, editor, "Cherokee Baskets."
214. Smith and Strickland, *Building One Fire*, 40.
215. Marriott Papers.
216. NARA.
217. Marriott Papers.
218. Quinlan, "Is Indian Basket Making Becoming a Lost Art?"
219. Marriott Papers.
220. Gregory, *Old Ways Live.*
221. Lombardi, "Basketmaking."
222. Olson, Introduction, "Cherokee Baskets," 7.
223. Lost Arts Project booklet.
224. *Keetoowah News*, 5.
225. Olson, Introduction, "Cherokee Baskets," 7.
226. Victory Papers.
227. Marriott Papers, Box 17, File 13
228. Anderson, "Indians Strive to Preserve Native Art of Basketry."
229. Masters, e-mail exchanges.
230. Marriott Papers, Box 17, File 13;
231. Ibid., Box 7, File 16.
232. Carl Albert Center Congressional Archives.
233. Ken Masters, www.cherokeeimages.com.
234. Flippo, "Cherokee Baskets."

235. Marriott Papers, Box 17, File 13.
236. Gettys, *Basketry of Southeastern Indians*, 31.
237. National Museum of the American Indian.
238. Klein, "Kenwood Artisans."
239. Olson, Introduction, "Cherokee Baskets."
240. Marriott Papers, Box 17, File 13.
241. Ibid.
242. *Lawrence Journal-World*, Septenber 10, 1995.
243. Gettys, *Basketry of Southeastern Indians*, 29.
244. Lombardi, "Basketmaking," 7.
245. Agard-Smith, *Southeastern Native Arts Directory*.
246. Lombardi, "Basketmaking."
247. Flippo, "Cherokee Baskets."
248. National Museum of the American Indian.
249. Indian-Pioneer Papers, recorded interview with George Duck, vol. 26.
250. Ibid.
251. Lost Arts Project booklet.
252. *Stilwell Democrat-Journal*, 1964 issues (April 9, September 10 and 17 and October 1).
253. Olson, Introduction, "Cherokee Baskets," 7.
254. Ibid.
255. Burke, provided copy of collections information.
256. Marriott Papers.
257. Cherokee Heritage Center.
258. Anderson, "Indians Strive to Preserve Native Art of Basketry."
259. Marriott Papers, Box 17, File 13.
260. Quinlan, "Is Indian Basket Making Becoming a Lost Art?"
261. Olson, Introduction, "Cherokee Baskets," 7.
262. Masters, www.cherokeeimages.com.
263. Burke, provided copy of collections information.
264. Quinlan, "Is Indian Basket Making Becoming a Lost Art?"
265. Coatney, provided list of baskets.
266. NARA.
267. Lost Arts Project booklet.
268. Chavez, "Cherokee Basket Maker Shares Her Talent."
269. Indian Arts and Crafts Board, *Baskets by Mavis Doering*.
270. *Stilwell Democrat-Journal News*, April 9, 1964.
271. Ibid., 1969.
272. Lombardi, "Basketmaking," 7.

273. Lost Arts Project booklet.
274. Field, *Art and Romance of Indian Basketry*, 30.
275. Burke, provided collections information.
276. Sturtevant, *Handbook of North American Indians*, 371.
277. Field, *Art and Romance of Indian Basketry*, 30.
278. Quinlan, "Is Indian Basket Making Becoming a Lost Art?"
279. Marriott Papers, Box 17, File 13.
280. Foreman, *Cherokee Weaving and Basketry*, 31.
281. Indian-Pioneer Papers, recorded interview with Millie Pigeon, vol. 71, 1937.
282. Anderson, "Indians Strive to Preserve Native Art of Basketry."
283. Lombardi, "Basketmaking," 7.
284. Unattributed published clippings in files of author.
285. Lombardi, "Basketmaking," 7.
286. Marriott Papers, Box 17, File 13.
287. Gregory, *Old Ways Live.*
288. Flippo, "Cherokee Baskets."
289. Sturtevant, *Handbook of North American Indians*, 371.
290. Marriott Papers, Box 17, File 13.
291. Ibid.
292. Power, *Art of the Cherokee.*
293. Wyckoff, *Woven Worlds.*
294. Indian-Pioneer Papers, recorded interview with Arlie Reeves, vol. 75.
295. NARA.
296. Ibid.
297. Conley, *Cherokee Encyclopedia*, 29.
298. Philbrook Museum of Art, collection record 1948.27.14.
299. Five Civilized Tribes Museum, collection record 1964.09.02 a & b.
300. Sturtevant, *Handbook of North American Indians*, 371.
301. Carl Albert Center Congressional Archives.
302. Burke, provided copy of Philbrook collections information of object 1948.39.162.
303. Ibid., object 1948.39.300.
304. Sturtevant, *Handbook of North American Indians*, 371.
305. Marriott Papers, Box 17, File 13.
306. Anderson, "Indians Strive to Preserve Native Art of Basketry."
307. Ibid.
308. Marriott Papers, Box 17, File 13.
309. Ibid.

310. Ibid.
311. Anderson, "Indians Strive to Preserve Native Art of Basketry."
312. Carl Albert Center Congressional Archives.
313. Power, *Art of the Cherokee.*
314. Anderson, "Indians Strive to Preserve Native Art of Basketry."
315. Indian-Pioneer Papers, recorded interview with Susie Washington, vol. 95, 1937, 370.
316. National Museum of the American Indian.
317. Burke, provided copy of Philbrook collections information of objects 1948.39.187, 1948.39.188 and 1948.39.189.
318. Ibid., objects 1946.47.8, 1948.39.68, 1948.39.171, 1948.39.175 and 1948.39.172.
319. Olson, Introduction, "Cherokee Baskets."
320. Marriott Papers, Box 17, File 13.

REFERENCE MATERIALS

Adair, James. *History of the Indians.* London: Edward & Charles Dilly, 1775, 424. Viewed at olivercowdery.com/texts/1775Adr1.htm.

Agard-Smith, Nadema. *Southeastern Native Arts Directory*. Bemidji, MN: American Indian Studies Press, Bemidji State University, 1993, 102, 104–5, 108.

Ancestry.com. Oklahoma and Indian Territory, Dawes Census Cards for Five Civilized Tribes, 1898–1914, and United States Federal Census and posted family records.

Anderson, L'vere. "Indians Strive to Preserve Native Art of Basketry." *Tulsa World*, September 8, 1940.

Anderson, Matthew. Personal communication, June 1, 2015.

Ataloa (Mary Stone McLendon). "The Revival of Indian Art in Oklahoma." In *Indians at Work.* Washington, D.C.: Office of Indian Affairs, June 15, 1937.

Ballenger Room, card file of Cherokee Seminary students, John Vaughan Library, Northeastern State University, Tahlequah, OK.

Bliss, Anne. *North American Dye Plants*. New York: Charles Scribner's Sons, 1980, 18.

Buffington, Loretta, basket maker, conversation with author, August 30, 2014, at Cherokee Heritage Center during Cherokee National Holiday.

Burke, Christina. Curator, Philbrook Museum of Art, Tulsa, OK. Personal communication with curator, August 4, 2014, regarding published error concerning an object in Philbrook Museum of Art collection. Provided copy of Philbrook Collections information, 2013.

Bushnell, David I. "The Sloane Collection in the British Museum." *American Anthropologist.* New Series 8 (1906): 678–79.

Cain, Shawna. "Buckbrush: A Cherokee Source for Basketry." *Cherokee Phoenix*, December 2009.

Carl Albert Center Congressional Archives: Wilburn Cartwright Photograph Collection, Box 9, Folder 2, and Elmer Thomas Photograph Collection, Box 16, Folder 2. University of Oklahoma, Norman, OK.

Chavez, Will. "Cherokee Basket Maker Shares Her Talent." Interview with Thelma Forrest. *Cherokee Phoenix*, July 22, 2014. www.cherokeephoenix.org/18113/Article.aspx.

———. "Cottrell Carries On Mother's Basket-Weaving Legacy." *Cherokee Phoenix*, December 2014.

Cherokee Arts Center and Spider Gallery, Tahlequah, OK. www.cherokeeartscenter.com.

Cherokee Heritage Center, Cherokee National Historical Society, Park Hill, OK. Collections list, 2013.

———. www.cherokeeheritage.org.

Cherokee National Treasures. www.cherokeeheritage.org/wp-content/uploads/2013/08/ProgramWeb.pdf.

Cherokee Nation, Tahlequah, OK. www.cherokee.org.

Cherokee Phoenix. "TCCO to Host Meeting, Basket Weaving Class." October 5, 2015.

———. "World's Tallest Cherokee Basket Nears Completion." April 18, 2012. www.cherokeephoenix.org/Article/Index/6178.

Chumwalooky, Carolyn. Interview with author, October 20, 2015, in Kenwood, followed by phone call, October 29, 2015.

CN file, used by Mickel Yantz, former exhibitions manager at the Cherokee Heritage Center, conducting research for exhibitions, clippings with two images concerning Miss Cherokee pageant of 1959. Copy received by author.

Coatney, Jackie. Curator, Delaware County Historical Society, Jay, OK. Provided list of baskets in collection, 2014.

Coats, Charlotte. "Hamburg Cane." Weaving the Cherokee Double Weave Basket. instructionscherokeebasket.blogspot.com/2005/09/hamburg-cane.html.

Coe, Ralph T. *Lost and Found Traditions*. Exhibition catalogue. Seattle: University of Washington Press, 1986, 85.

Conley, Robert J. *Cherokee.* Photographs by David Fitzgerald. Portland, OR: Graphic Arts Center Publishing, 2002, 46–47.

———. *A Cherokee Encyclopedia*. Albuquerque: University of New Mexico Press, 2007, 29, 152, 160, 262.

Cottrell, Vivian. www.basketsbyviv.wix.com.

Craig, Marilyn. "Cherokee Heritage Center Presents History Woven in Art Exhibit." *Gaduwa Cherokee News*, 2012, 1.

Crews, C. Daniel, and Richard W. Starbuck, eds. *Records of the Moravians Among the Cherokees*. Vol. 4. Tahlequah, OK: Cherokee Heritage Press, 2012, 1474.

Culin, Stewart. *Games of the North American Indians.* Washington, D.C.: Bureau of American Ethnology, 1907, 105.

Debo, Angie. *And Still the Waters Run.* Princeton, NJ: Princeton University Press, 1940, 6.

Devlin, Jeanne M. *Oklahoma Today*, November–December 1990, 23; December 1991, 5.

Duggan, Betty J., and Brett H. Riggs. *Studies in Cherokee Basketry*. Knoxville, TN: Frank H. McClung Museum, University of Tennessee, 1991, 27, 29, 41.

Duvall, Deborah L. *The Cherokee Nation and Tahlequah.* Charleston, SC: Arcadia Publishing, 1999, 54.

Emerson, Sue Ann. *The Houstons of Tahlequah.* Dallas: Copper Press, 1994, 249.

Everett, Dianna. "Fairs." Oklahoma Historical Society, www.okhistory.org.

Fariello, M. Anna. *Cherokee Basketry: From the Hands of our Elders.* Charleston, SC: The History Press, 2007, 41, 92.

———. Personal communication via e-mail, July 23, 2015.

Faulk, Odie B., and Billy M. Jones. *Tahlequah, NSU, and the Cherokees.* Tahlequah, OK: Northeastern State University, 1984, 107.

Field, Clark. *The Art and Romance of Indian Basketry*. Tulsa, OK: Philbrook Art Center, 1964, 8, 25, 27, 30.

Five Civilized Tribes Museum. www.fivetribes.org. Also notation on collection item card file for 1964.09.02A&B, Muskogee, OK.

Flippo, Jody, ed. "Cherokee Baskets & Basketmakers." *Cherokee Quarterly*, Summer 2000, 13–18.

Foreman, Carolyn Thomas. *Cherokee Weaving and Basketry*. Muskogee, OK: Star Printing, 1948, 21, 30–31, 33.

Foreman, Grant. *Indian Removal.* Norman: University of Oklahoma Press, 1972, 230–31, 261, 287.

Foster, Ken. Provided a tour of Kenwood and discussed Cherokee Nation educational programs and people he worked with in the 1970s. October 20, 2015.

Foster, Ted. This resident of Chelsea provided a presentation at Pocahontas Indian Women's Club, Claremore, attended by the author, March 23, 2013.

Fredrick, Terra Coons. "Cherokee Baskets of Oklahoma Origin" (Clark Field Collection Philbrook Museum), a study completed March 16, 1989, basically a compiled list of the baskets at Philbrook with gathered notes. Author talked with her in 2013.

Gettys, Marshall, ed. *Basketry of Southeastern Indians*. Idabel, OK: Museum of the Red River, 1984.

———. Conversation with author, March 23, 2013.

———. *Southeast: Woven Worlds*. Tulsa, OK: Philbrook Museum of Art, 2001, 189.

Goshorn, Shan. Brochure titled *Shan Goshorn Studio* listing website, www.shangoshorn.com, 2015.

Gregory, H.G., ed. *The Old Ways Live.* Natchitoches, LA: Williamson Museum, Northwestern State University, 1990, 91, 95, 96.

Hill, Sarah H. Correspondence in file of object NAM-13-08-005, Sam Noble Oklahoma Museum of Natural History, University of Oklahoma. Posted June 1992.

———. "Marketing Traditions: Cherokee Basketry and Tourist Economies." In *Selling the Indian: Commercializing & Appropriating American Indian Cultures*, edited by Carter Jones Meyer and Diana Royer. Tucson: University of Arizona Press, 2001, 212, 223.

———. "Weaving History: Cherokee Baskets from the Springplace Mission." *William and Mary Quarterly*, 3rd series, 53, no. 1 (January 1996): 115, 129–30.

Holiday, Billie. Song lyric, 1939. www.billieholiday.com.

Indian Arts and Crafts Board. *Baskets by Mavis Doering*. Anadarko, OK: IACB's Southern Plains Indian Museum and Crafts Center, 1980.

———. www.iacb.doi.gov.

Indian Education Hearings, Study of the Education of Indian Children. Ninetieth Congress. Washington, D.C.: Government Printing Office, 1969. National Archives Records Administration, Fort Worth, TX.

Indian-Pioneer Papers. Works Progress Administration in Division of Archives and Manuscripts, Oklahoma Historical Society, Oklahoma City, OK, and Western History Collections, University of Oklahoma Libraries, Norman, OK, 1937. Recorded interviews with Martin Blackwood, vol. 8; Rachel Dodge, vol. 25; George Duck, vol. 26; Lucinda Hickey, vol. 42; Jennie Hines, vol. 42; Ellen Shanon Magee, vol. 60; Dorothy Field

Morgan, vol. 64; Millie Pigeon, vol. 71; Arlie Reeves, vol. 75; Susie Washington, vol. 95.

James, George Wharton. *Indian Basketry*. 4th ed. New York: Henry Malkan, 1909.

Johnson, Joyce. *Cherokee Baskets*. Tulsa, OK, 1983.

Joplin Globe, October 6, 1966, and June 1, 1971.

Keetoowah News, November 2006, 5. hopkinsmusic.net/pdf/2006_keetoowah.pdf.

King, Duane, and David Fitzgerald. *The Cherokee Trail of Tears*. Portland, OR: Graphic Arts Books, 2007, 11, 70.

Klein, John. "Kenwood Artisans Thriving/Small Settlement Attracting National Attention." *Tulsa World*, March 31, 1990.

Laughlin, Patricia. Online biography of Alice Lee Marriott, Oklahoma Historical Society.

Lawrence (KS) Journal-World, September 10, 1995.

Lawson, John. *History of Carolina*. London, 1714, 189.

Lemaster, Aaron. "Cherokee Baskets & Basketmakers." *Cherokee Quarterly*, 2000, 24.

Lombardi, Betty Ritch. "Basketmaking Among the Oklahoma Cherokees: Revival, Adaptation, Continuation." *Mid-America Folklore* 16, no. 1 (Spring 1988): 5, 6, 7, 8, 9.

Lost Arts Project booklet. www.cherokeeheritage.org/wp-content/uploads/2013/08/ProgramWeb.pdf.

Mankiller, Wilma. Profile of Cherokee statesman John Ketcher, *Cherokee Phoenix*, December 6, 2006.

Marriott, Alice. Papers, Western History Collections, University of Oklahoma Libraries, Norman, OK, 1937. Box 7, Files 15 and 16; Box 15, File 5; Box 17, File 13; Box 77, File 11.

Mason, Otis Tufton. *American Indian Basketry*. 1904. Repr., New York: Dover Publications, 1988, 292.

Masters, Ken. E-mail exchanges with author, October 2015, and website at www.cherokeeimages.com.

McDaniel, Herman. "Vann Slaves Remember." Murray County Museum, 2003. www.murraycountymuseum.com/vann.html.

Meredith, Mary Ellen. Account of family recollections told to author in 2012.

Miami (OK) Daily News, December 1959, 10.

Mihesuah, Devon A. *Cultivating the Rosebuds*. Champaign: University of Illinois Press, 1993, 31.

Mirro-Krome. *Indians of the Southwest*. San Bruno, CA, n.d.

Mooney, James. *Myths of the Cherokee*. Nashville, TN: Cherokee Heritage Books, 1982, 179, 241.

Morgan Friedman investment corporation. "The Inflation Calculator." www.westegg.com/inflation.

Mullins, Jonita. "Horse Races Were Highlight of Spaulding Park Fair." *Muskogee (OK) Phoenix*, March 29, 2008.

Murphy, Jami. "Sequoyah Indian Weavers Hall Needs Makeover." *Cherokee Phoenix*, April 6, 2009. cherokeephoenix.org/Article/Index/2716.

National Archives and Records Administration (NARA). Photo captions and photographs included in annual reports of Extension Work, Five Civilized Tribes, Muskogee, Record Group 75, 1937, 1941 and 1944. Southwest Region NARA, Fort Worth, TX.

National Museum of the American Indian. Collections records provided to author, July 2014, available online.

Native Plant Information Network. www.wildflower.org.

New Castle (PA) News, October 27, 1969, 30.

O'Brien, Mary. "Cherokee Baskets & Basketmakers." Part 2. *Cherokee Quarterly*, 2000, 15, 16, 21.

Oklahoma Department of Forestry. www.forestryok.gov. See Ecoregions.

Olson, Betsy P. Introduction, "Cherokee Baskets & Basketmakers." *Cherokee Quarterly*, Summer 2000, 7.

Power, Susan. *Art of the Cherokee: Prehistory to the Present*. Athens: University of Georgia Press, 2007, 48, 57, 87, 147, 206–8, 209, 249.

Quinlan, Lula Egan. "Is Indian Basket Making Becoming a Lost Art?" *Tulsa World*, May 12, 1957.

Reed, Matt. American Indian collections specialist at Museum of Oklahoma History, Oklahoma City. List of Oklahoma Cherokee baskets provided to the author, November 4, 2015.

Reed, Sarah. "Cherokee Weaver Helps Recreate Lost Artifacts, Dying Art." *Marshall (MO) Democrat-News*, February 29, 2012. www.marshallnews.com/story/1820813.html.

Roastingear, Kathryn. E-mail sent to author listing basket makers selling works at the Cherokee Heritage Center, Park Hill, Oklahoma. September 8, 2014.

Sallee, Marilyn. "Don't Trip on the Devil's Shoestring." Native Plant Society of Texas, February 9, 2011. npsot.org/wp/story/2011/1679.

Sam Noble Oklahoma Museum of Natural History, Ethnology Department, University of Oklahoma, Norman, OK. Research object data in catalogue number NAM-13-08-012.

Sattler, Richard. "Baskets of the Cherokees." In *Basketry of Southeastern Indians*, edited by Marshall Gettys. Idabel, OK: Museum of the Red River, 1984, 29, 32.

Sequoyah Indian Weavers. *International Textile Exposition* booklet, June 1947. Cherokee Heritage Center archives, Park Hill, OK.

Smith, Chadwick Corntassel, and Rennard Strickland. *Building One Fire*. Tahlequah, OK: Cherokee Nation, 2010, 40.

Smithsonian Institution, online collections research, National Museum of Natural History. Item number E399875-0.

Speck, Frank G. "Decorative Art and Basketry of the Cherokee." *Bulletin of the Public Museum of the City of Milwaukee*, 1920.

Starr-Scott, Barbara. Former Cherokee council member. Telephone conversation with author, 2013.

Stilwell Democrat-Journal, online archives at www.newspapers.com: 1960 issue (August 29), 1964 issues (April 9, September 10 and 17 and October 1), 1968 issues (February 15, 4, and April 25, 2), 1969 issue and 1973 issue, Stilwell, OK.

Stremlau, Rose. *Sustaining the Cherokee Family: Kinship and the Allotment of an Indigenous Nation*. Chapel Hill: University of North Carolina Press, 2011, 221.

Sturtevant, William C. *Handbook of North American Indians*. Vol. 14, Southeast. Washington, D.C.: Smithsonian Institution, 2004, 371.

Swearingen, Scott. Videographer, *Cherokee Basket Maker.* Tulsa, OK, 1990.

Taylor, Linda. E-mail sent to author with list of basket makers selling work in the Cherokee Nation Gift Shop at the tribal complex south of Tahlequah, OK. August 4, 2014.

Thornton, Russell. *The Cherokees: A Population History*. Lincoln: University of Nebraska Press, 1990, 44.

Timothy, John. Ataloa Lodge, Bacone College, Muskogee, OK, from research visit in 2013.

Tulsa World. "Chelsea Woman Aids Cherokee Weavers in Marketing Wares." April 7, 1935.

———. "SA Auxiliary Bids Farewell to Liaison." June 11, 1991.

Turnbaugh, William, and Sarah Turnbaugh. *Indian Baskets*. West Chester, PA: Schiffler Publishing, 1986, 98, 100, 106.

Twin Territories Magazine. Advertisement for Hudson's Book Store, July 1903, Muskogee Public Library archives, Muskogee, OK.

University of Oklahoma, Elmer Thomas Collection, Carl Albert Congressional Archives, Norman, OK. Photo no. 1794.

University of Tennessee. Penelope Johnson Allen Collection, Special Collections Library, Knoxville, TN. Spoliation Claim of John Vann, Folder 171, Box 2033, dated September 29, 1838.

Victory, C.C. Papers, Sequoyah Indian Weavers Association, Cherokee Heritage Center archives, Park Hill, OK.

Watts, James D., Jr. "Basket Beauty." *Tulsa World*, February 10, 2013, D3.

———. "Tulsan Shan Goshorn Earns Fellowship Honor." *Tulsa World*, November 19, 2015, D2.

Western History Collections, Doris Duke papers. Vol. 14, interview with Lula Hair, University of Oklahoma, 1969.

White, Max E. "Anthropologists and the Eastern Cherokee." In *Anthropologists and Indians in the New South*, edited by Rachel Bonny and J. Anthony Paredes. Tuscaloosa: University of Alabama Press, 2001, 12.

Wicker Woman. www.wickerwoman.com.

Woodward, Grace Steele. *The Cherokees*. Norman: University of Oklahoma Press, 1963, 7.

Wright, Muriel H. "American Indian Corn Dishes." *Chronicles of Oklahoma*, Oklahoma Historical Society, Oklahoma City, 1958, 157.

Wyckoff, Lydia L. *Woven Worlds: Basketry from the Clark Field Collection at the Philbrook Museum of Art.* Tulsa, OK: Philbrook Museum of Art, 2001, 13, 19, 23, 28–29, 225–26, 229.

Yale Peabody Museum of Anthropology, New Haven, CT. Online catalogue.

INDEX

D

E

F

G

H

I

J

K

T

U

V

W

Y

BASKETS

Fingers, Little People,
Making their magic—
Transforming material.

A basket contains holy space
Where fingers, at cross-currents,
Have webbed material.

In that culture-containing space
Secrets have been stirred
By ladles of experience.

Basket makers need only
Talk to their fingers
To hear the mysteries.

—Karen Coody Cooper

First published in 1985 in *Artifacts* 13, no. 3, American Indian Archaeological Institute, Washington, CT.

ABOUT THE AUTHOR

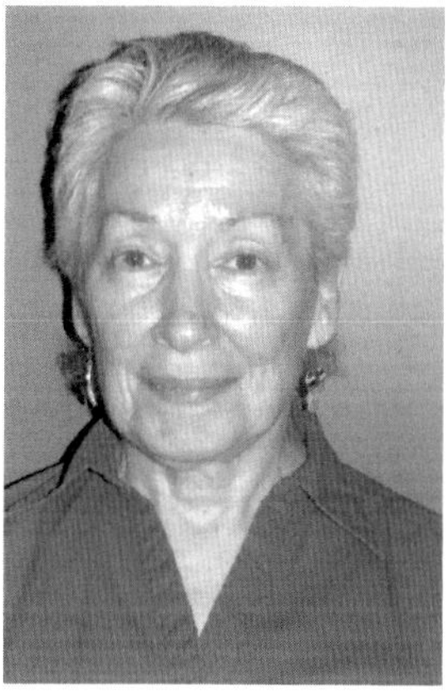

Karen Coody Cooper, now living in Tahlequah, Oklahoma, was born in Tulsa in 1946 as Karen Korliss Rollins and grew up in Collinsville. Her grandmother Callie Coody was enrolled as a child on the Dawes Roll and became a hardworking farm wife near Texanna, Oklahoma, close to her allotment in the former Canadian District of the Cherokee Nation. Callie's grandfather was a son of Jane Ross, elder sister of John Ross, principal chief of the Cherokee before Removal and throughout the Civil War in Indian Territory. Cooper chose a museum career and retired from the National Museum of the American Indian in 2007, the same year her first book, *Spirited Encounters: American Indians Protest Museum Policies and Practices*, was published by AltaMira Press. She also wrote *Cherokee Wampum: War and Peace Belts, 1730 to Present* and *Woodchuck Meets Algonquian Cousins*, published by soddenbank press. Her poetry volume, *Fault Line: Vulnerable Landscapes*, was named the 2010 Best Book of Poetry by the Oklahoma Writers Federation.